WALKING

WENSLEYDALE

HILLSIDE GUIDES - ACROSS THE NORTH

Long Distance Walks
•COAST TO COAST WALK   •DALES WAY   •CUMBRIA WAY
•WESTMORLAND WAY •FURNESS WAY •LADY ANNE'S WAY •PENDLE WAY
•BRONTE WAY   •CALDERDALE WAY   •NIDDERDALE WAY

Circular Walks - Yorkshire Dales
•WHARFEDALE   •MALHAMDALE   •SWALEDALE   •NIDDERDALE
•THREE PEAKS   •WENSLEYDALE   •HOWGILL FELLS
•HARROGATE & WHARFE VALLEY   •RIPON & LOWER WENSLEYDALE

Hillwalking - Lake District
•LAKELAND FELLS - SOUTH   •LAKELAND FELLS - EAST
•LAKELAND FELLS - NORTH   •LAKELAND FELLS - WEST

Circular Walks - Lancashire/Cumbria
•BOWLAND   •PENDLE & THE RIBBLE   •WEST PENNINE MOORS
•ARNSIDE & SILVERDALE   •LUNESDALE

Circular Walks - North Pennines
•TEESDALE   •EDEN VALLEY   •ALSTON & ALLENDALE

Circular Walks - North East Yorkshire
•NORTH YORK MOORS, SOUTHERN   •HOWARDIAN HILLS

Circular Walks - South Pennines
•ILKLEY MOOR   •BRONTE COUNTRY   •CALDERDALE

Short Scenic Walks - Full Colour Pocket Guides
Yorkshire Dales
•UPPER WHARFEDALE   •LOWER WHARFEDALE   •MALHAMDALE
•UPPER WENSLEYDALE   •LOWER WENSLEYDALE   •SWALEDALE
•NIDDERDALE   •SEDBERGH & DENTDALE
•RIBBLESDALE   •INGLETON & WESTERN DALES
Northern England
•HARROGATE & KNARESBOROUGH   •ILKLEY & WASHBURN VALLEY
•AIRE VALLEY   •AMBLESIDE & LANGDALE   •BORROWDALE
•BOWLAND   •AROUND PENDLE   •RIBBLE VALLEY
•HAWORTH   •HEBDEN BRIDGE

*Send for a detailed current catalogue and price list
and also visit www.hillsidepublications.co.uk*

WALKING COUNTRY

———

WENSLEYDALE

Paul Hannon

———

Hillside

HILLSIDE
PUBLICATIONS
20 Wheathead Crescent
Keighley
West Yorkshire
BD22 6LX

First published 1987
Fully Revised 4th edition 2011

© Paul Hannon 1987, 2011

ISBN 978-1-907626-06-7

Cover illustration: Aysgarth Falls
Back cover: Middleham Castle; Semerwater; West Burton
Page One: At Aysgarth
Page Three: Redmire Force
(Paul Hannon/Hillslides Picture Library)

The sketch maps in this book are based upon
1947 Ordnance Survey One-Inch maps
and earlier Six-Inch maps

Printed in Great Britain by
Carnmor Print
95-97 London Road
Preston
Lancashire
PR1 4BA

CONTENTS

WALKING COUNTRY - WENSLEYDALE

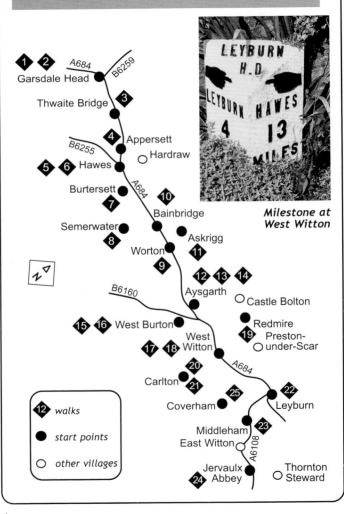

Milestone at West Witton

◆1 ◆2 **A684** **B6259**
Garsdale Head

Thwaite Bridge
●3

●4 Appersett
B6255
◆5 ◆6 Hawes ○ Hardraw

Burtersett **A684**
●7 ●10
Bainbridge
Semerwater ●
◆8 ●11 Askrigg
Worton ●
◆9 ◆12 ◆13 ◆14
Aysgarth ○ Castle Bolton
B6160
● Redmire
◆15 ◆16 West Burton ◆19 Preston-
West ○ under-Scar
◆17 ◆18 Witton ● **A684**
◆20
Carlton ◆22
◆21 ◆25 Leyburn
Coverham ●
◆23
Middleham
East Witton ○ **A6108**
Thornton
Jervaulx ○ Steward
◆24 Abbey

◆12 *walks*

● *start points*

○ *other villages*

INTRODUCTION

Wensleydale is the very heart of the Yorkshire Dales, a broad green valley with innumerable hidden features that more than make amends for any lack of instant grandeur. Here one must make an effort to seek out the attractions, and the ensuing pages lead the discerning walker to a host of splendid sights. An oft-made claim that this is Yorkshire's major dale is a point that Wharfedale would surely debate, unless the many side-valleys and the fertile pastures downstream of the National Park boundary are included. These lesser valleys are something unique to Wensleydale, for Coverdale, Walden, Bishopdale, Raydale and several more are all sizeable dales in their own right. Each contributes to the Wensleydale scene. Further down-valley meanwhile, a further wealth of walking country is explored in the *Ripon & Lower Wensleydale* book.

The individuality of the valley is also exhibited by its name, this being the only major dale not to take its title from the river. The Ure - anciently the Yore, a name still applied in some quarters - lost out to the village of Wensley which lies just outside the Park on the road to Leyburn. This the Dales' most fertile valley was once a great hunting forest, and other associations with history involve a Brigantes' hill-fort, Iron Age lake dwellings, a Roman road, a Roman fort, a 13th century abbey, a 14th century castle, a 15th century fortified manor house, a 16th century beacon site, a 17th century hall, and traces of lead and coal-mining and of quarrying. Not bad for starters!

The natural attractions deserve a mention now. It will be noticed that not many walks take in the riverbank, for a good deal of its course is without rights of way: the river itself leads an uneventful life other than one or two famous moments which all who have visited the dale will already know. Neither are the high tops very inviting to the genteel rambler, indeed the bulk of Wensleydale's walking is to be had somewhere between the two extremities. The physical structure of the dale provides a series of regular ledges on which some superb walking can be found. These mid-height terraces also generally provide the best views. The crowning glory of Wensleydale however (despite the Ure's general lack of interest) is the waterfalls. Nowhere else can boast such a fine array of tumbling falls, for most of the numerous side valleys also proudly possess their own force. These are the gems that make Wensleydale special.

Access to the countryside

The majority of walks in this guide are on public rights of way with no access restrictions. Walks 1, 5, 7, 9 and 17 also make use of Right to Roam. This freedom allows more logical routes to be created, and on most days of the year you are free to walk responsibly over these wonderful landscapes. Of various restrictions the two most notable are that dogs are normally banned from grouse moors; and also that the areas can be closed to walkers for up to 28 days each year, subject to advance notice being given. Inevitably the most likely times will be from the 'Glorious Twelfth', the start of the grouse shooting season in August. It is, however, unlikely that any of the modest adventures in these pages will impinge on any such activity. Further information can be obtained from the Countryside Agency (see opposite), and ideally from information centres. Finally, bear in mind that in springtime, avoiding tramping over open country away from paths and tracks would help to safeguard the most crucial period for vulnerable ground-nesting birds.

Getting around

A very good public transport service runs through Wensleydale, with the principal one of several bus routes travelling along the valley to Hawes from Leyburn, connecting numerous villages. As they incorporate many of the start points, it is possible to link any number of these walks into linear routes, often creating a longer ramble, and at the same time keeping your car off the road.

Aysgill Force, Gayle

8

Using the guide

Each walk is self contained, with essential information being followed by a concise route description and simple map. Dovetailed in between are notes and illustrations of features along the way. Snippets of information have been placed in *italics* to ensure that the essential route description is easier to locate. The sketch maps serve merely to identify the location of the routes rather than the fine detail, and whilst the description should be sufficient to guide you around, an Ordnance Survey map is strongly recommended.

To gain the most from a walk, the detail of the 1:25,000 scale Explorer map is unsurpassed. It also gives the option to vary walks as desired, giving an improved picture of your surroundings and the availability of linking paths. The first-named map covers most of the walks in this book, ably supported by the other two:

- *Explorer OL30 - Yorkshire Dales, North/Central*
- *Explorer OL19 - Howgill Fells/Upper Eden Valley*
- *Explorer 302 - Northallerton & Thirsk*

Also useful for general planning are Landranger maps 98 and 99.

USEFUL ADDRESSES

Yorkshire Dales National Park
Hebden Road, Grassington, Skipton BD23 5LB • 01756-751600

Information Centres
National Park Centre, Station Yard
Hawes • 01969-667450
National Park Centre,
Aysgarth Falls • 01969-663424
Central Building, Railway Street,
Leyburn • 01969-828747

Yorkshire Dales Society
Town Hall, Settle BD24 9EJ
• 01729-825600

Open Access
Helpline • 0845-100 3298 *or*
www.countrysideaccess.gov.uk

Public Transport Information
Traveline • 0870 608 2608

Moorcock Inn, Garsdale Head

HELL GILL

START *Garsdale Head   Grid ref. SD 797926*

DISTANCE *7¹4 miles (11¹2km)*

ORDNANCE SURVEY MAPS
1:50,000
Landranger 98 - Wensleydale & Upper Wharfedale
1:25,000
Explorer OL19 - Howgill Fells/Upper Eden Valley

ACCESS *Start from the Moorcock Inn at the junction of the Kirkby Stephen road with the Hawes-Sedbergh road. Roadside parking. Garsdale station on the Settle-Carlisle line is a mile away.*

A bracing upland walk, and a real treat for railway enthusiasts

From the strategically sited Moorcock head a few strides along the Kirkby Stephen road and take a bridle-gate on the right, from where a hard path crosses rough pasture to join a farm drive at a stone-arched bridge. *The drive uses a parallel modern crossing, while the old bridge looks down on a lovely little waterfall on the youthful Ure.* Across, turn left on a branch track upstream: it rises away to quickly drop back, though one could simply remain on a lower path. *Wild Boar Fell looks impressive ahead, with Lunds Viaduct just to the left.* Soon joining the drive to Blades at a bridge, follow it right to the hamlet. Don't enter but bear right to a stile into a small enclosure. Over a stile just ahead turn right along the fence to a gate accessing a corner stile. Now rise left on a moist green track through reeds, swinging more uphill to a gate in the wall above. Now ascend a more welcoming sheep pasture, through a gate left of an old barn then more steeply to a gateway at the top to rise to the derelict farm of High Dyke. Use gates to its right to gain the open fell, and the old track known as the High Way.

The High Way is part of the route taken by Lady Anne Clifford on visits to her Westmorland castles in the 17th century. It long formed the major 'highway' from Hawes to Kirkby Stephen until the arrival of the turnpike road - the present road turning off at the Moorcock - in 1825. Though the High Way is steeped in history, its one perpetual feature is the improving prospect of majestic Wild Boar Fell across the valley: looking back over Garsdale Head, Whernside exerts its full stature. High Dyke was an inn catering for travellers on this old road: an old limekiln stands just ahead.

Turn left alongside the intake wall, running a marginally downhill course for more than two miles to Hell Gill Bridge. *Several lively ravines are crossed, one by the surviving barns at what was High Hall.* When the wall finally drops away the track runs on to the last gorge before Hell Gill Bridge. *This is the infant Ure, little more than a mile from its birth high on Lunds Fell.* The way continues to

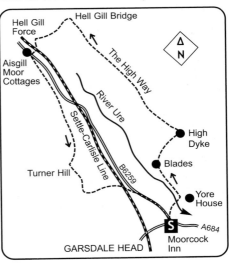

quickly reach Hell Gill Bridge. *This single-arched structure straddles an unexpected gem. The beck, source of the Eden, rushes through a deep, dark and narrow ravine. The old Yorkshire-Westmorland border (and modern equivalent) follows it down to the road: the National Park shares this boundary.*

Across the bridge turn immediately left over a stile to descend a faint grassy track to the cottage of Hell Gill, then continue down the drive through the fields. Part way down it bridges the bubbly beck before reaching a sharp bend left towards a railway bridge just ahead. First, however, be sure to deviate right a few strides for a dramatic appraisal of Hell Gill Force. *This splendid waterfall makes a vertical drop over a cliff, particularly impressive in view of the infancy of the stream: youngsters should be on a tight rein here.* Crossing the railway bridge, the road is joined at Aisgill Moor Cottages. *This is the first of the walk's two crossings of the famous Settle-Carlisle line. Just south of the cottages is Aisgill Summit, at some 1169ft/356m the highest point on a main line in Britain.*

Go briefly left, and across a bridge on the right a thin path crosses rough ground to a bridle-gate at a wall corner. With never more than an intermittent path, and numerous moist moments to face, go left with the wall, commencing a near-straight course bound for the distant barns of High Shaw Paddock. Quickly passing through a gate, a lone tree on the right stands over a pothole. As the wall briefly departs amid limestone surrounds, keep straight on to be quickly rejoined by it after a gate ahead. The wall remains faithful now as the next gate sends you off along a large pasture to ultimately reach High Shaw Paddock. At the barns don't use the gate ahead but pass through two gateways to the right, and follow a wall away to a gate onto rough moorland. A faint trod heads away to enter reeds: evade the bulk of these by locating a contouring path bearing right, soon starting to slant up the steeper slope. This distinct old way can be traced to the head of a deep grassy ravine. From the limestone rocks here you'll see a wall ahead: don't cross to it but rise further, slanting only gently left to merge with the wall on the brow, at a gate in a fence descending from Swarth Fell.

Follow the wall left over the dome of Turner Hill. *The walk's summit at 1525ft/465m is an excellent viewpoint, its fine surround of fells including Swarth Fell, Wild Boar Fell, Cross Fell, Great Dun Fell, Mickle Fell, High Seat, Lunds Fell, Widdale Fell, Ingleborough, Whernside, Great Coum, Baugh Fell and The Calf, with Cautley Crag. Wensleydale stretches away beneath Wether Fell and Addlebrough all the way to Penhill.* Continue down the wallside to cross it at a gate/stile just past a small dip. *Look back over the gate to see Yarlside in the Howgills appearing.* Heading away, diverge from a wall on the left to descend a reedy pasture to a prominent footbridge over the railway. A stile gives access alongside a house at South Lunds. Across, its drive heads away to join the road by a former school. The Moorcock is only a short half-mile along to the right. *Almost at once an old milestone is passed on the right.*

GRISEDALE

START *Garsdale Head   Grid ref. SD 787917*

DISTANCE *5^{1}4 miles (8^{1}2km)*

ORDNANCE SURVEY MAPS
1:50,000
Landranger 98 - Wensleydale & Upper Wharfedale
1:25,000
Explorer OL19 - Howgill Fells/Upper Eden Valley

ACCESS *Start from the railway station on the Settle-Carlisle line. Parking on the road climbing from the main road to the station.*

> *An unglamorous stroll through a bleak Dales upland - great!*

    Garsdale Station is an isolated spot, known as Hawes Junction when the Wensleydale branch existed. It is well placed for a day on the lonely fells where the valleys of Garsdale, Wensleydale and Mallerstang form, sending the rivers Clough, Ure and Eden to very different points of the compass. The Clough merges into the Rawthey and in turn the Lune to reach the sea at Morecambe Bay, the Ure joins the Ouse and flows into the North Sea via the Humber, while the Eden remains independent all the way to the Solway Firth. Descend to the main road and cross to a stile. Head straight up the wallside, and when it turns away rise left to a stile a little beyond a gate. A thin path rises gently away across the moist Garsdale Low Moor, crossing to meet an impressive drop to the gorge of Grisedale Beck as it prepares to become the River Clough. *Prominent across it are the stone men on Grisedale Pike, a shoulder of the immense Baugh Fell. Looking back out of the dale, Whernside asserts a shapely profile.*

    The lovely waterfall of Clough Force can be appraised by a short detour left down along the rim. From the next stile hovering above the drop, the path continues, soon using a prominent tree as a guide towards the cottage at Blake Mire. *The dome of Swarth Fell rises across Grisedale ahead.* Bear right to find a gate/stile further along, then a path bears right across drier terrain, fading at a wall gap beneath a barn to cross to a stile revealing more of the valley. A winding grass track drops down to the photogenic ruin of Rowantree at the bottom. Cross the emerging stream on a slab bridge to a stile left of the ruins, then cross an access track to rise to a gate left of the barn ahead. Advance on to meet the narrow valley road at Moor Rigg. *Grisedale is a hidden valley brought to public attention by a 1970s TV documentary highlighting the demise of its farms.*

Cross straight over, a stone slab on a trickle points to a stile between spread gates. Cross the field to a gate/stile at the far bottom corner, then slant down to join the beck. Follow it upstream a short way, and as it swings left advance to a gate/stile onto the

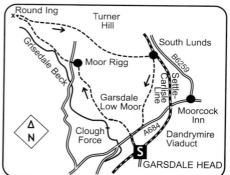

drive to the renovated Reachey, beneath a sprawling plantation. Cross straight over, across a few slabs and to the field end on your left, where a gate/stile put you back on to the bank of the beck. A nice little path runs between chirpy stream and wall, emerging at the end to leave the beck and advance straight on between denser reeds (left) and steeper bank (right). A little further, cross a track and rise left up the reedy bank to look down on the tree-shrouded former farms of East and West Scale, now merely a barn and a ruin.

From here forge a little further up the curving valley, rising gently through reeds to trees marking the location of Round Ing. *Extensive remains suggest this was once a farmhouse of substance.* From the walk's turning point double sharply back across the sloping pasture to reach an old wall corner, and continue across to locate an old stile in the crumbling wall ahead. Heading away, bear left to merge onto a track rising left the short way to the barn of Flust. Here a better track is joined: go right through gates, crossing a stream beneath trees, and after a short pull it runs an improving course atop the intake wall. *This grand stride runs on past an old limekiln, with Ingleborough and Whernside seen beyond Grisedale.*

Further on, the track meets the valley road as it loses its surface on gaining the moor. Don't turn down but keep straight on a grassy track remaining above the intake wall. *Fell ponies graze in happy profusion hereabouts.* As the wall kinks a little right the fading track forges on a parallel course: as the wall kinks again, the green way passes through an old boundary: here leave it and swing gently up to the left, revealing a stile over the wall ahead. *Wensleydale stretches ahead all the way to Penhill, while closer to hand are Wild Boar Fell and High Seat.* Cross and head away, diverging from the wall on the left to descend a very reedy pasture to a prominent railway footbridge at South Lunds. A stile gives access alongside a renovated house. Don't cross, but from a stile between the line and the house head diagonally away on a thin trod down to a collapsed wall. *Lunds Viaduct is just to the left.* A nice trod climbs slightly left up grassy moor, on through a dip between gentle slopes to locate a stile in the wall ahead. *You now have a good view of Dandymire Viaduct.* The trod drops slightly to a stile ahead, then down to a dip and up to a gate/stile in a fence. Descend one final

pasture to a stile back onto the main road opposite cottages at Mudbecks. The starting junction is two minutes to the right.

Clough Force, Grisedale

THE HIGH WAY

START *Thwaite Bridge   Grid ref. SD 826922*

DISTANCE *6³4 miles (11km)*

ORDNANCE SURVEY MAPS
1:50,000
Landranger 98 - Wensleydale & Upper Wharfedale
1:25,000
Explorer OL19 - Howgill Fells/Upper Eden Valley

ACCESS *Start from a large lay-by alongside the bridge on the A684 midway between Appersett and the Moorcock Inn.*

> *A largely easy walk, mixed pastures on the outward leg contrasting with long return strides on an ancient highway*

Cross the bridge to Thwaite Bridge Farm and turn into the yard. Almost at once take a gate on the right and bear away to a stile in the corner beyond. Advance with a fence to a stile ahead then away with the wall, taking a gap-stile in it part way along. Resume along the foot of a larger pasture, and on above a group of trees. As the wall drops away keep straight on an intermittent path past a low ruin to reach a stile in the far corner, above a few more trees. A little path runs on through rough pasture to the base of Cotterside Plantation. *The playful Ure winds down below: across it are the vast slopes of Widdale Fell, while Baugh Fell forms the skyline ahead*. From the stile advance straight on an intermittent trod, meeting a track at the end. Through a gate it fords a stream and runs on as a fine green way, fading and slanting slightly down to meet a wall leading along to Yore House. Behind the farm is a stile beneath a small wood. *Around this point Wild Boar Fell makes its presence known by joining its companion Swarth Fell ahead, and will remain the finest feature of the view for some time.*

Cross the pasture to a wall-stile just below the base of Cobbles Plantation, then drop to join a track near the youthful Ure. Follow this upstream the short way to join the drive to Blades at a bridge, and follow this right to the hamlet. Don't enter the yard but bear right to a stile into a small enclosure. The stile just ahead marks a path junction. *WALK 1 has a more direct route up to the High Way.* Go immediately left between pens towards the buildings, but again avoid them by a gate on the right into reedy pasture. From the minor brow just ahead the right of way performs a dog-leg, bearing left down to a footbridge on the Ure, then doubling back across the pasture to pass through a gateway in a fence to locate a corner stile in the wall just behind. Don't look for the two tiny strips of woodland shown on the map, they don't exist. Now go left above the wall, a moist section that ends at a corner stile. In improved terrain a thin trod ascends to a stile visible in the wall ahead.

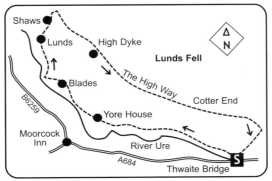

Cross the minor brow of Cowshaw Hill to reveal Lunds Chapel below, descending to a stile to gain access. *Dating from the late 17th century, this humble place of worship has a bell-cote. A few scattered gravestones still stand, and the view to Wild Boar Fell remains as fine as when it was built.* From a stile behind it cross an old stone slab bridge on Scars Gill and bear right to a stile into a derelict farmyard. From a stile at the top ascend steeply via a footbridge to a stile above. A steep pull above Scars Gill's wooded ravine sees you approach Shaws. *The former Garsdale Head Youth Hostel opened in 1949 and closed in the early 1980s: this was a fine*

17

'getaway' spot, and its demise remains a sad loss, particularly as the Lady Anne's Way long-distance walk virtually passes its door. Continue up to a footbridge over the gill beneath a fine waterfall. A flight of mossy steps leads to a gate above the house alongside further impressive gill scenery. Go left above the confines of Shaws, and at the corner take the distinct green rake curving up and tracing a wall up to a choice of stiles onto the High Way.

Here the return leg commences with contrastingly simple instructions: turn right on the path and just stay on it for some $2^1\!2$ miles! The way never strays more than a few strides from the intake wall: no height is lost, though the way continually gains a little more. *The High Way is best known as part of the route taken by Lady Anne Clifford on visits to her Westmorland castles in the 17th century. Now a route for more leisurely travellers, it had for many centuries formed the major 'highway' from Hawes to Kirkby Stephen until the arrival of the turnpike road - the present road turning off at the Moorcock Inn in 1825. Only building passed is the forlorn ruin of High Dyke, once an inn: an old limekiln stands to your left. Largely grassy moor rises to unassuming Lunds Fell. Virtually all this section is a joy to tread, the going improving further on lush limestone turf. Long strides are matched by long views of high country in this remote corner of the National Park: Whernside and Great Coum form a distinctive pairing beyond Garsdale Head, while there is a brief appearance of the Howgill Fells between Baugh and Swarth Fells. Opposite are Widdale Fell's broad shoulders, while Dandrymire Viaduct is well seen as the last mile of the old Wensleydale line curves in to join the Settle-Carlisle line.*

The walk's high point at some 1640ft/500m is only gained on arrival at Cotter End. *By now the full length of Wensleydale leads past Wether Fell and Addlebrough to a backdrop of Penhill.* Here the way finally winds down past a fine limekiln. *Over to the left the mass of Great Shunner Fell slides into place from valley to summit above lonely Cotterdale.* Just below is a pair of gates: from the left one (bridle-gate) trace the old way down the wallside until reaching a stile in the wall. Cross it and contour away across a reedy pasture, and then down across an old grassy track to the top of a slender strip of woodland. From a stile in the wall there a clearer little path drops down another large pasture to a stile into trees, where a path drops down to return to the start.

4

MOSSDALE & COTTERDALE

START Appersett   Grid ref. SD 858906

DISTANCE $7^1 4$ miles ($11^1 2$km)

ORDNANCE SURVEY MAPS
1:50,000
Landranger 98 - Wensleydale & Upper Wharfedale
1:25,000
Explorer OL19 - Howgill Fells/Upper Eden Valley

ACCESS Start from the green. Park considerately alongside, near the bridge, or just across it.

Two secluded valleys are linked by a short rougher section, with all the major tops around the dalehead on show

Appersett is a small farming community, the first settlement of such size in Wensleydale. It stands where Widdale Beck joins the main river. From the green cross the road bridge on Widdale Beck, and after a big limekiln and some barns take a stile on the left. Walk parallel with the road as far as New Bridge on the Ure, then turn to follow the river up-dale. Quickly reaching a stile, the little path is deflected from the bank along a wooded slope, soon emerging to run to a stile ahead. Here vacate the river by rising to a wall corner, then on above trees to a stile. Bear right across a hollow to a stile in a section of wall, then on a little further to a stile into the trees. A path drops to cross a sidestream as it enters the Ure, then bear left to a gate by a barn. Continue straight on a wallside to join the drive going left towards Birkrigg. *Cotter End shows a shapely profile.*

When the drive forks right up to the farm, keep left on the level branch through several pastures. *Up to the left is the distinct course of the railway that carried the branch line from Hawes to Garsdale Head (then Hawes Junction) on the Settle-Carlisle line.*

When the drive swings left to climb through a low scar to Mid Mossdale, instead take a moist little path right beneath the diminishing scar. Later improving, it runs to a bridle-gate at the end to emerge back alongside the Ure. Resume a pathless but pleasant stroll upstream, linked by gates through several pastures. In the second you might miss the confluence that means from hereon you are shadowing Mossdale Beck rather than the Ure. Later entering a field where Mossdale Head Farm appears just ahead, leave the beck and strike across to it. Through a gate, pass right of the main building to a gate accessing the yard, and go right to the bridge over Mossdale Beck. *Upstream are two sets of lovely waterfalls, the upper ones being beyond the four-arched viaduct.*

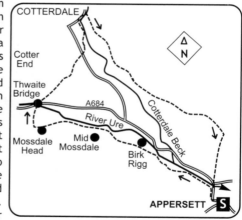

Across the farm bridge take a gate in front with another just behind, and a grassy track climbs the field to a gate where fence and wall meet. Through it go right with the wall, and as it loops right go straight ahead on a faint way to rejoin it to descend to a stile onto the main road at Thwaite Bridge. Cross straight over both road and bridge, and head up a little path through the trees. From a stile at the top a slender path climbs the steep pasture, aiming for the top edge of the trees to your right. Over the stile continue less obviously over a gentler brow, bearing right and easing out to contour across to a stile in a wall ahead. *The best views of the walk are to be had while crossing this broad ridge under Cotter End, looking down the length of Wensleydale to a distant Penhill: at 1245ft/380m this is the highest point of the walk.*

From the stile cross the parallel High Way path and on over mixed ground to a wall-stile ahead. Passing through newly planted trees to reveal Cotterdale ahead, the moist path descends via a fence-stile to the unfenced access road. Don't cross the cattle-grid but drop to a fence-stile below, then left through an old wall to drop to a level pasture by the beck. Go left to a stile right of a barn, then advance to a footbridge on West Gill. *On your right here is the confluence where West and East Gills form Cotterdale Beck.* From the bridge bear right to a corner stile by East Gill, and follow its enclosed course upstream to the road in Cotterdale. *This cosy hamlet stands in its own little valley, sheltered by broad ridges coming down from Lunds Fell and Great Shunner Fell.* Turn briefly right, still with East Gill for company: between the last clusters of buildings leave by a footbridge to cross the fields by gap-stiles. After a tiny watercourse leads to the third stile, cross it then trace it along a field bottom as far as another crossing. Ignore this and strike left up a green rake to a stile at the top above a clump of trees.

This is the start of a superb, sustained near-level ramble along the valley flank. A little path turns right just above the wall to a stile by a barn, then across to a gateway, fading above an island barn before rising to a stile into Black Rash Wood. *Scattered trees have been joined by new plantings among the bracken, with lush turf, isolated rocks and a spoil heap above. Here also you look down on a sharp bend of the beck backed by Cotter End.* On leaving maintain the contour to a gate, behind which are the crumbling wall patterns of Kempera Folds. A much longer pasture follows, and towards the end a distinct groove slants left up towards an old wall corner: keep right of a short length of wall just beyond to contour round to a wall-stile ahead. From it a path contours again to join a broad track. *Here you make brief acquaintance with the Pennine Way during its long climb to Great Shunner Fell.* Turn down it to become enclosed at a gate/stile. *During this last section the three giants on the south side of Wensleydale (Wether, Dodd and Widdale Fells) fill the scene, with Ingleborough sneaking in behind.*

Forsake the track at the first gate on the right, and drop down by a wall to a corner stile. Initially dropping steeply, cross to the far end of this large field to find a gate at the end. Pry House Farm is down to the right. Drop to another gate below, then aim for a stile in front of roadsigns which indicate arrival at the Hardraw junction of the A684. Go left on the main road, crossing New Bridge to a stile on the right to re-enter Appersett as you began.

5

HARDRAW FORCE

START *Hawes   Grid ref. SD 875898*

DISTANCE *6 miles (9$\frac{1}{2}$km)*

ORDNANCE SURVEY MAPS
1:50,000
Landranger 98 - Wensleydale & Upper Wharfedale
1:25,000
Explorer OL30 - Yorkshire Dales, North/Central

ACCESS *Start from the National Park car park in the old station yard. Served by bus from Leyburn. •Open Access, see page 8.*

A superbly varied walk with extensive views across Wensleydale

Hawes is the 'capital' of upper Wensleydale, a lively, colourful town to which all visitors are drawn. The place gains even greater character at its Tuesday market, when there are as many locals in evidence as tourists. An unconventional layout retains a cobbled road, and a leisurely exploration is essential. Once the last stop on the Wensleydale branch line, its station has been put to use as a National Park Centre. Also keeping the station yard alive is the Dales Countryside Museum. Two surviving industries are today also tourist attractions. The absorbing ropemakers is at the old station entrance, while the creamery is found on the Gayle road. This long established business was on the verge of disappearing in 1992, along with many jobs, but a management buyout secured its future and its popularity has since soared. Milk from the cows you see on your walk is used in the production of the celebrated Wensleydale cheese. From seeing the cows munching the grass to nibbling the finished product, you can enjoy the whole experience! St Margaret's church dates from 1851, and there is a modern youth hostel on this major staging post on the Pennine Way.

From the car park take the path by the old railway bridge up onto the road, and turn right to follow it out of town (footway). Within a minute an access road goes left, and with it a gate signals the route of the Pennine Way, whose flagged course is followed to rejoin the road a little further on. Cross Haylands Bridge over the Ure, then take a stile which soon appears on the right, a sketchy path crossing the field to an impressive stone-arched bridge. *Already, Addlebrough, Crag, Yorburgh and Wether Fell are seen back across the valley.* From the bridge a path climbs half-right to a stile on the brow just above, from where a large field is crossed to a stile in the top corner. Cross straight over the road to a stile opposite, and resume the rise in the same direction to a stile ahead. Two further stiles quickly ensue before a steep climb to another in the top-right corner. Turn right along the narrow road to Sedbusk.

Tiny Sedbusk is an unspoilt hamlet looking across the dale to Hawes and beyond from an airy altitude of little under 1000ft/300m. It is so laid back it has even avoided the back road from Hardraw to Askrigg, and is accessed only by a narrow lane. Reaching a junction by a Victorian postbox turn left into its confines, noting a lovely old Primitive Methodist

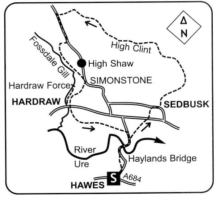

Chapel of 1875, now a private house. Head up the lane between the houses, and at the top end of the green bear right as the enclosed track of Shutt Lane takes over to climb away. *This slants up the hillside with superb views across the valley.* Immediately before a gate where it starts to run free, take a gate on the left from where a sunken way slants up a field. When it turns off a path continues up to a tiny plantation, above which it slants left to a gate in a wall. The path then runs to a gate onto the open fell: up to the right is an old limekiln.

Continue up the track left of a low scar, but quickly break off to ascend easy slopes at the eastern end of High Clint above. Now head left for a superb ramble on faint ways atop the craggy scarp. *This enjoys extensive panoramas over upper Wensleydale's wide surround of 2000ft fells. Up to your right, meanwhile, Lovely Seat sits way back but is not a great deal higher.* After almost a mile a prominent cairn to the right at 1752ft/534m overlooks a splendid pair of stone men. As the scarp has now largely abated ignore its lesser, higher continuation ahead, and instead advance straight on from the beacons, descending tussocky ground in line with a large stone sheepfold ahead. Drop onto a grass track on this lower shelf, and go right beneath the folds: on your left is the more modest Low Clint. Remain on this edge until it fully fades, then slant gently down to a cattle-grid visible on the Buttertubs road at Sowry Head.

Turn down over the grid and descend as far as a gate/stile at a parking verge on the right, where a grass track doubles back to a barn. From a gate/stile behind it descend the wallside to a stile at the bottom corner. A path drops down a wooded bank at a bend of Fossdale Gill, and out at the bottom it runs briefly with the beck. From a stile on the left leave it and cross several fields via gates and/or stiles, a straight line to approach High Shaw. Don't enter the yard: instead a little path deflects you right to steps down onto an access road. Turn right down this as far as a caravan site entrance, then take a small gate on the left into wooded Fossdale Gill. After

seeing the waterfall a short way up, a flagged path accompanies the beck downstream: an early footbridge offers a choice of banks, and below two low falls a second footbridge is reached. Here leave the beck to prepare itself for its big moment, to be witnessed from below: a tall-walled path rises left to the road.

Pub sign at Hardraw

Opposite: Hardraw Force

Go briefly right, and with Simonstone Hall (public bar) in front, take a drive on the right. Over a cattle-grid/stile to a brow, it drops through two fields to West House Farm. From a stile to its right a path descends two more fields to emerge via a yard into Hardraw. *This tiny hamlet is made famous by its waterfall, claimed to be the highest single drop above ground in England. It also has its own church, St Mary & St John (1881) and a tearoom.* Access to Hardraw Force is through the Green Dragon Inn, where a charge is made to view the spectacle: it is but a 5-minute walk into the increasingly impressive amphitheatre. *More so than most, the tiny beck needs to have seen recent rain for the scene to be fully appreciated. The cliff over which the water spills is Hardraw Scaur, or Scar. In the gorge below the force, band contests have made a welcome revival - the old bandstand is passed on the way.* Back at the pub take a track opposite to a kissing-gate set back, from where an initially flagged path sets off through the fields. On losing its flags keep straight on to a kissing-gate at the end, then advance on a couple of wallsides to a stile onto a road. Turn right, dropping down to pick up the outward route, over Haylands Bridge and back into Hawes.

6

AYSGILL FORCE

START Hawes   Grid ref. SD 875898

DISTANCE 5³4 miles (9km)

ORDNANCE SURVEY MAPS
1:50,000
Landranger 98 - Wensleydale & Upper Wharfedale
1:25,000
Explorer OL2 - Yorkshire Dales South/West **or**
Explorer OL30 - Yorkshire Dales, North/Central

ACCESS Start from the centre. National Park car park in the old station yard. Served by bus from Leyburn.

A stroll in the valley of Gayle Beck, and two lovely villages

For a note on Hawes see page 22. Leave through the small main street car park almost opposite the Board Inn. From a stile in its left corner a path rises half-right across two fields to join the Gayle road. Turn left past the creamery into the heart of the village. *Delightful Gayle was here long before its big brother came on the scene. Solid stone cottages fan out along lanes from the little arched bridge, on either side of which Gayle Beck tumbles over a series of ledges. Downstream is Gayle Mill, restored in 2004: built in 1785 as one of the earliest textile mills, it served a variety of uses and last worked in 1988. Gayle Institute occupies a former chapel dating from 1755, next to a burial ground of earlier origin.*

After leaning on the bridge take the short cobbled way to the right, continuing along a lane to an old iron kissing-gate after the last house on the left. Climb half-right past a wall corner to a stile at a junction with the Pennine Way: your return route comes through here, though you don't really tread the same ground. *Wether Fell rises to the left, with Dodd Fell straight ahead.*

26

Continue at the same angle to a stile above the deep wooded gill before descending to its bank. The way now shadows Gayle Beck all the way upstream to Aysgill Force. Storms have caused a landslip to devastate one short section which can hopefully be circumvented. *Aysgill Force is an impressive waterfall into a deep, wooded bowl, one of the valley's lesser-known falls.* Above comes an immediate contrast as things open into the gentle upper section of the valley. Remain with the beck past two footbridges, the second by West Close Barn (this comes after successive ladder-stiles see a wall deflect you from the beck). Through a gate/stile at the end of the next field, rise right to join a farm track at a gate. Through it is a junction: double back right through rough pastures.

As you gain a little height Lovely Seat slightly overtops High Clint ahead, with Great Shunner Fell to the left. Becoming enclosed and better surfaced it runs on to a cluster of barns, then drops down more firmly to become surfaced at a barn on a bend: just yards further a stile on the right sees you join the Pennine Way. Head away to a gap-stile, then on to one used earlier in the walk. Here turn left to accompany a wall down through two fields onto a lane. Almost immediately take another road joining it to drop down onto the edge of Gayle. Passing the large house of Rookhurst and the departure of the Pennine Way, keep straight on past the Methodist Church of 1833 and back to the bridge. This time cross and take the left branch.

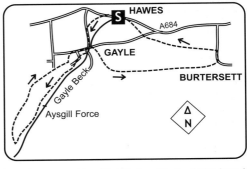

Immediately after the attractive Old Hall with its 1695 lintel on the right, take a stile into a field and climb to a small gate on the brow. Bear left to a stile by the top corner. *You now enjoy big views of the encircling fells: Yorburgh and Wether Fell rise above, while Dodd Fell, Widdale Fell, Swarth Fell, Lunds Fell and Great Shunner Fell all feature.* Continue through a further one before easing out in the next field. From a stile left of a gate bear left to another, then on to a barn by the head of a wooded gill. From the path junction here a virtual straight line takes you to Burtersett: a string of gap-stiles, usually alongside gates, lead along this distinct shelf past numerous barns, ultimately reaching an impressive barn where a cart track forms. This grassy wallside way soon becomes enclosed as Shaws Lane, at which point Burtersett appears ahead. The walled track runs unerringly on into the top of the village.

Burtersett is an attractive little village set well back from the valley floor, and also peacefully above the main road through the dale. Most of the dwellings cluster round a rising lane and a tiny green. Turn left a short way down the street, and pass alongside a former Wesleyan chapel of 1870 into a field. A flagged path runs to a stile ahead, then forks. Take the surfaced right branch which slants down the field to meet a level path. Go left on its straight, flagged course through several stiles. At another fork your flagged way bears right again, on past a barn and through more stiles to emerge onto a back road. A few strides left is a stile opposite, and from one behind it a flagged path resumes across one final field to emerge at the far corner onto the road on the edge of Hawes. Turn left on the footway past the auction mart back into the centre.

At Gayle

WETHER FELL

START Burtersett   Grid ref. SD 890892

DISTANCE 5$\frac{1}{2}$ miles (9km)

ORDNANCE SURVEY MAPS
1:50,000
Landranger 98 - Wensleydale & Upper Wharfedale
1:25,000
Explorer OL30 - Yorkshire Dales, North/Central

ACCESS Start from the village centre. Park by the bend at the top. Leyburn-Hawes buses use the main road. •Open Access, see page 8.

> *A well-defined climb and a bracing stroll along a Roman road*

Burtersett is a small village set well back from the valley floor, and also peacefully above the main road through the dale. Most of the dwellings cluster round a rising lane, with a former Wesleyan chapel and a tiny green. From the green at the top of the village, take the 'no through road' branching off the road corner alongside the Institute. Almost at once it forks, and your track climbs left, leaving the last cottage behind to cross a tiny stream to a gate. The firm track embraces a steep slope and remains easy to follow as it scales the hillside, always sloping right. *By the first gate big views look across the dalehead. Lovely Seat just overtops High Clint, followed anticlockwise by Great Shunner Fell, Lunds Fell, Wild Boar Fell, Swarth Fell, a section of Howgill Fells and Widdale Fell: below is Hawes.* At the next gate the track becomes less harsh and starts to ease out a little. *You are looking right down on Gayle and Hawes, while Wether Fell itself appears ahead, set back but not too much higher.* Meeting the next wall it swings uphill with it: continue straight up when it turns off, gaining equal height with the upthrust of Yorburgh across to the left. Ignore a lesser right fork to a gate and continue up to finally transform into a grass track. Levelling out at a wall corner, it makes a delightful crossing of a shelf to a gate ahead near a wooden shed.

Beyond it the track winds grandly up the fell-side as a sunken green way. *You are now looking back down over Yorburgh, and further along to Crag, Addlebrough and Penhill.* Ignoring lesser branches, the track levels out and runs mercurially along to the last gate of the climb as you enter the high moor-land of Wether Fell. *The unseen summit, however, is set considerably well back,*

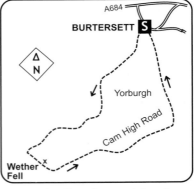

defended for now by deep peat groughs. Though a track heads on, your way virtually at once forks right on a better continuation which remains close by the wall on the right. The summit quickly reveals itself some way ahead, but this rather more circuitous course should not be hastily abandoned: your path is heading ever nearer the top, and the temptation to strike out left should be avoided until the slope there becomes invitingly steep.

Grand level strides lead past an old quarry on Flint Hill to be greeted by new views west as Dodd Fell joins the array of dalehead fells. A little further the way makes an insignificant descent with the wall a little lower still: through moister terrain you pass the site of further old workings. At a slight apex of the wall, alongside a sinkhole, the ground ahead starts to drop away again to moister ground, while steeper slopes alongside confirm it's time to leave. Climbing briefly left things level out at a small peat castle, and this reveals the summit cairn only a couple of minutes beyond. A level grassy trod completes a relatively dry ascent. *Wether Fell is the only Wensleydale climb to 2000ft: the dale's other mountains are set much further back and constitute a far greater challenge. The summit is known as Drumaldrace, and is probably as good a view-point for the surrounding Dales mountains as anywhere.*

To begin the return head down the only significant drop past a reedy pool to quickly join the broad track of Cam High Road just to the south. *The secluded valley of Raydale is seen below, including the hamlet of Marsett. Cam High Road is the Roman road from Ribblehead to the Bainbridge fort. The whole of that section forms an exhilarating high-level march that can still be trod today. Though 'improved' further westward, several miles still remain to provide a gem of a walkers' route.* The old road is now followed left for some time on its gentle descent eastwards to Bainbridge. *Crossing a slight brow reveals Semerwater beneath Addlebrough.*

The way soon becomes enclosed by walls, and whilst you could simply remain on it, for greater variety leave beyond a sharp bend, where a gate sends a bridleway right. A grassy track heads away, soon swinging left to slant gently down to a guidepost marking a cross-paths. Keep straight on the inviting, level green bridleway along this broad ridge to a gate/stile in a wall ahead. Further, through an old wall, the way soon forks: keep left to another way-marked crossroads. This time go left on the near side of the old wall, a thin path running beneath it and a limestone scar to a gate in a wall. Wensleydale returns ahead, and a grassy way drops down and across to a gate/stile back onto the Roman road.

Cross straight over to another gate/stile, and a slender green path heads away, down to a stile by a gate just across a stream. *Yorburgh is at its shapeliest now above you.* The path enjoys a pleasant, direct descent of this large pasture to a stile left of a wall corner, again a short way beyond another small stream. *Just a few strides over the brow Burtersett is revealed, with Hawes and the dalehead fells beyond.* Passing through an old wall a steeper drop through reeds improves to slant more faintly left down through a large pasture to a stile at the foot of a plantation. Drop slightly left through successive stiles, and then follow the right-hand wall through the last field to re-emerge in Burtersett.

The summit cairn, Wether Fell

SEMERWATER

START *Semerwater   Grid ref. SD 921875*

DISTANCE *5 miles (8km)*

ORDNANCE SURVEY MAPS
1:50,000
Landranger 98 - Wensleydale & Upper Wharfedale
1:25,000
Explorer OL30 - Yorkshire Dales, North/Central

ACCESS *Start from the lake foreshore near the bridge. Fee payable at Low Blean - see signs.*

> *An easy lake circuit with a colourful fellside climb*

Semerwater was the largest lake in Yorkshire's North Riding, and in a district not endowed with sheets of water it is a popular venue for both birdlife and watersports. Near the lakefoot is the Carlow Stone, dropped by a giant, but the best-known legend of the district relates how an inhospitably treated visitor caused a whole 'city' to disappear under the waters. Rather more certain is that Iron Age lake dwellings existed here. From the foreshore head along the road away from the bridge (not over it), and at Low Blean Farm at the foot of the hill take a gate/stile on the right. Maintain a level course through the fields, taking in several stiles to one by a barn. A good path now drops down toward the lakeshore, though at an early stile it quickly angles away from it again.

From a step-stile a good path slants gradually upwards across the rough pastures of Yorkshire Wildlife Trust's Semerwater reserve above the head of the lake. From a stile at an information panel, slant up around a wall corner enclosing trees and along a wallside through a gate/stile to arrive above the remains of Stalling Busk's old church. *A stile accesses the ruin, stood in isolation some 200 feet below the hamlet. Originally dating from 1603, it was rebuilt in 1722 and abandoned in 1909. The ruins romantically overlook the lake, and exude an atmosphere not felt at the replacement St Matthew's up by the houses.* Just beyond it pass through a gate/ stile, where the path forks. Go left on an improving path rising by a small, tree-lined stream: this old churchgoers' way rises to a gate at the top, then up a fieldside to a gate/stile on the edge of Stalling Busk. Continue on the short-lived farm track to a junction at a hairpin bend, where a slim path ascends open ground to emerge onto the cul-de-sac road in the hamlet. *This peaceful farming settlement enjoys views of the lake from its hillside perch. Nearby Raydale Preserves offers refreshments in season.*

Go right just as far as the church, and at the sharp bend take the rough, enclosed track of Busk Lane down to the right. Though this enclosed way can be followed all the way down to a ford on Cragdale Water, a nicer option awaits. Vacate the

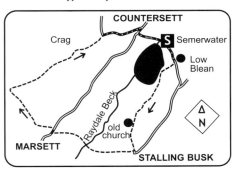

lane part way down at a stile on the right just beyond gates either side, and head down the steep pasture. *Improved views include Marsett beneath Crag.* At the bottom continue close by the right-hand wall, crossing it at a stile towards the end to follow its other side to a stile at the very end. Behind it is a footbridge on Cragdale Water to rejoin your old way, now a stony track. Bear right on this, quickly crossing larger Raydale Beck at a ford/footbridge, a little beyond which it becomes enclosed by walls. The going improves as Marsett Beck is joined to lead pleasantly along to the hamlet, bearing right across its green to the road. *The workmanlike green is focal point of this sequestered farming hamlet. Above the lake this valley is known as Raydale, this being the central, largest and only level one of three valleys which merge between Marsett and Stalling Busk: Bardale and Cragdale are the lesser two.*

Cross the green to the road bridge, and turn right over it. Ignoring an access road left, advance a little further and double back left on an enclosed rough lane. Shortly after it starts to rise take a gate in the fence on the right and follow the wall away, rising to a wall-stile across the top. Resume on an improving green path, veering right of a tiny stream and the wall, and ascending more steeply through Marsett Cow Pasture. Easing out it passes through a fence-gate, with a pocket wood up to the right. Another steeper pull leads to a ladder-stile over the intake wall onto open fell, and an inviting path ascends steeply again. *Addlebrough enjoys a grand spell beyond the lake.* Gradually the path eases out, crossing a green track and along to a path crossroads at an old gateway. *Big views ahead reveal a skyline including Wether Fell with its Roman road, Yarlside in the Howgill Fells, Swarth Fell, Yorburgh in front of Wild Boar Fell, Lunds Fell, Great Shunner Fell and Lovely Seat.*

Turn right and follow the path close by the crest. *Addlebrough returns to view: don't worry about the lake, that will soon return in style.* It runs on through a gate then gains the true skyline to reach a distinctive limestone-capped knoll. *At around 1666ft/508m this is the walk's summit, with big views north across Wensleydale to Great Shunner Fell and Lovely Seat.* Just past it another gate brings the entire lake dramatically into the scene. Here the path departs the ridge by slanting down to the right, passing beneath a limestone scar and slanting mercurially down the flank above a small wood. At the bottom pass through a gate by sheep pens and cross right to the next gate, the green track then winding down and left to a gate onto Crag Side Road. This drops to a staggered junction on the edge of Countersett: go a few strides right then drop down the steep road to cross Semerwater Bridge to finish.

The old church, Stalling Busk

9

ADDLEBROUGH

START Worton   Grid ref. SD955900

DISTANCE 6¼ miles (10km)

ORDNANCE SURVEY MAPS
1:50,000
Landranger 98 - Wensleydale & Upper Wharfedale
1:25,000
Explorer OL30 - Yorkshire Dales, North/Central

ACCESS Start from the village centre. Roadside parking by the bridge or a lay-by just past the pub. Served by Leyburn-Hawes bus.
•Open Access, see page 8.

> *A splendid ascent of a shapely fell, with outstanding views*

Worton is a small collection of dwellings along the valley road, but still has the time-honoured Victoria pub (1698 date-stone). Note also a house dated 1729 bearing an inscription above a side window: 'MICHAEL SMITH MECHANICK BUT HE THAT BUILT ALL THINGS IS GOD Heb 3'. From the centre either of two roads lead up onto the main road. In between these turn up the side road signed to Thornton Rust. At a hairpin bend turn right into the farming hamlet of Cubeck and then immediately left through a gate, from where a walled track climbs steeply away. At the left-hand of two gates the track runs more freely. *Good views look across the valley, with Askrigg well seen opposite.* The track slants up past an old quarry, then up to a gateway at the top corner. *At this point on Worton Pasture, Addleborough appears directly above.* Behind the gate the track fades: cross to a gate over to the right after which the way picks up again to resume its level course, bearing slightly left to cross to another gate at a wall junction. *Ahead are Yorburgh, Wether Fell, Crag and Widdale Fell.*

Through the gate follow a wallside track to the far end of this moorland pasture, with Addlebrough waiting above. This ultimately runs to a gate onto Carpley Green Road. *Just before this you are greeted with an outstanding prospect of Semerwater in its great bowl.* Just short of the gate, turn up the wallside rising towards the shapely prow. An intermittent trod rises gently away, remaining close by the wall until parting slightly before fading on steeper ground nearer the top: here rejoin the wall at the isolated Devil's Stone. *This large boulder was hurled by the Devil at Addlebrough's giant during a dispute.* The final stage is on steep grass that demands caution if wet as you veer left to use an obvious break in the band of low limestone cliffs. Above, step over a low fence to gain the plateau.

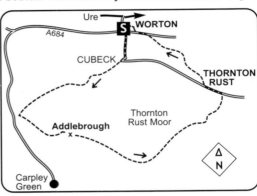

Now you can fully savour the view you have had for a while of Semerwater in its deep bowl of fells. Much closer, on a plateau just beneath the cliffs to the south (over the wall) is a bird's-eye picture of an Iron Age Brigante settlement, highly discernible even to the untrained eye. With a sturdy wall to your right, go briefly left past a solitary cup-marked rock and then follow the crest of the craggy northern escarpment along to a distinct mound on the top. *This is the site of a Bronze Age burial cairn marked by a small group of rocks: one is particularly well embellished with the cup-marks of these ancient people. Amid them the concrete base of an insensitively sited Ordnance Survey column is still evident. At 1575ft/480m Addlebrough is a classic table-topped fell that crops up in many Wensleydale views, and its own views over the dale are unsurprisingly excellent: Askrigg is particularly evident directly opposite.*

Continue away eastwards, soon bearing right to a ladder-stile part way along the wall ahead: just before it stands a cairn. A thin path heads away to a slight brow looking down on the flat expanse of Thornton Rust Moor. *The richly wooded lower dale stretches far beyond, featuring Bolton Castle and of course Penhill.* The path slants pleasantly down to a small clump of limestone rocks, where bear right to a nearby wall corner. Rising with the wall it quickly bears off left, over a minor brow where it improves further to drop gently to a stile in a wall below. Just a few steps further it joins the Carpley Green-Thornton Rust bridleway. Turn left on its grassy course to a gate/stile from where it heads off across the moor. With odd moist moments it swings gently right, through a dip and over a brow to drop to an intake wall gate off the moor. It then descends a reedy pasture to enter the walled confines of Moor Lane in the bottom corner, which leads unerringly down into Thornton Rust. *This lovely village is strung narrowly along a quiet lane, like many others in the dale free from the bustle of the valley floor. It has a mission attached to Aysgarth church, an Institute of 1924 (in memory of four villagers lost in the Great War) and numerous attractive dwellings.*

Go left along the road to the very edge of the village, and at the de-restriction sign take a gate on the right, dropping to a stile just below. A path runs left through slender woodland beneath a limestone scar, dropping down a few steps to a lower path then left a few strides to a stile out into a field. Here the final leg begins, a pathless trek through green pastures linked by stiles. Bear half-left to one in an outer wall corner, which sets the general course for an undulating slant that gradually loses height. Beyond a fence-stile cross to a wall-stile near a corner, with two more in quick succession before dropping to one hidden in a wall lined by trees. *Nappa Hall is well seen across the river.* With the main road just below, a change of angle sees you bear left on a parallel course through more fields. Emerging from a tree-filled enclosure with an oft-dry stream bear right towards a barn, and from a stile beyond it bear right to a corner stile onto the road. Go left with caution, and just after the pub take a stile on the right. A thin path slants down to the field corner, where a snicket runs on to the end of the village street. *Dale Farm House bears a 1691 datestone.* At the end turn right back down to the bridge.

RIVER BAIN

START *Bainbridge   Grid ref. SD 933901*

DISTANCE *5³4 miles (9km)*

ORDNANCE SURVEY MAPS
1:50,000
Landranger 98 - Wensleydale & Upper Wharfedale
1:25,000
Explorer OL30 - Yorkshire Dales, North/Central

ACCESS *Start from the village centre. Ample parking alongside the greens. Served by Leyburn-Hawes bus.*

A steady ramble by the shortest river and on an ancient highway

Bainbridge is a lovely village whose houses stand well back from an enormous green. Though the main road cuts across it, its effect seems insignificant. Most noticeable features are the stocks which still grace the green, and the Rose & Crown which is always in sight. Dating back several centuries, it is possibly the oldest in the dale. The structure which gives the village its name is itself centuries old, having been widened in 1785: it is a shapely plat-form from which to see not only the best stretch of the river, but the only part before it sneaks quietly round the back of the houses.

Brough Hill, peering over the houses at the east end, is the site of the Roman fort Braccium, while Norman lords based their foresters here, when the Forest of Wensleydale was a popular hunting ground. At the inn can be seen a horn blown at nine o'clock during winter months to guide benighted travellers to safety. Its origin goes back earlier still, as a warning sound in the days of the forest. This ancient event survives as a quaint custom. The village has shop, tearoom, butcher, garage, WCs and a quoits pitch on the green. There is a former Independent Chapel of 1864 with bell and *clock in place, the old school of 1875 on the green, a temperance hall of 1910, and an old Quaker Meeting House. Where your walk re-enters the village is a house that was once the 'Old Dame School', where over a century ago, pupils could learn the 'three R's' for 2d a week (that's 1p to you youngsters!).*

Leave by the Aysgarth (main) road at the corner of the green, crossing the bridge over the River Bain and climbing the steep hill. Take a slim stile on the right just before a junction and head across the pasture, keeping well above the steep drop to the river. *This gives good views over the village.* For a while parallel with the adjacent road, the path rises away, passing left of an 'island' field before levelling out. *The odd first*

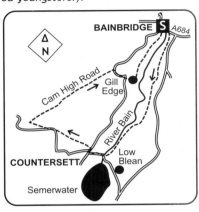

glimpse of Semerwater finds it below you! Along a brow the path runs on to the right-hand of adjacent stiles. With Semerwater now fully in view, a good path heads away. It fades as you commence a gentle decline above a steeper bank to your right down towards the river. Dropping to a corner stile ahead, advance on through stiles linking a couple of fields to drop down a larger pasture to a gate/stile. Here bear right to finally join the now adjacent river-bank. Its pleasant course offers a simple walk upstream to emerge onto the road at Semerwater Bridge. *Joining the Ure at Bainbridge, the Bain is claimed to be the shortest river in the country, a point which the Dibb, in Wharfedale would challenge.*

Before crossing it, have a potter along the lakeshore itself: its foot is directly in front. *Semerwater was the largest lake in the old North Riding of Yorkshire, and in an area not endowed with sheets of water, it is a popular venue both for birdlife and watersports. At the lakefoot is the Carlow Stone, said to have been dropped by a giant. The best-known legend of the district relates how an inhospitably treated visitor caused a whole 'city' to be submerged*

39

under the waters. Rather more certain is that Iron Age lake-dwellings existed here. Resume by crossing the bridge to climb the steep road to a staggered crossroads at Countersett. *This stage gives splendid views over the lake.* This small hamlet has a Friends' Meeting House of 1710 alongside a lovely old hall dating from 1650, also with strong Quaker connections. The steep slopes above command a superb panorama of Semerwater's side-valley, Raydale: best feature is Addlebrough across the valley.

Turn right for the hamlet, but before the first house opt for a rough access road to cottages on the left. Taking a gate on the left by the first dwelling slant steeply right to a brow, with a stile and tree-lined stream behind. A little path climbs left of a barn then slants left to a stile in the ascending wall. It then slants diagonally towards a wall opposite, but turns uphill before it to rise through a nick to a stile in the wall at the top. *At this point the Semerwater scene is finally lost: the brow of Crag frowns above you.* Follow the wall on your left along and up to a gate onto the Countersett-Burtersett road at its highest point on Hawes End. *At around 1360ft/415m this is also the summit of the walk, giving big new views to the upper dale backed by the 2000-footers of Swarth Fell, Wild Boar Fell, Lunds Fell, Great Shunner Fell and Lovely Seat.*

Semerwater   ***Opposite: River Bain***

Go right for a couple of minutes to a stile on the right, from where a thin path slants away gently left. Crossing a collapsed wall maintain this steady slant down the expansive reedy pasture to a stile onto a walled rough lane, Cam High Road. *Approaching it, Wether Fell and its outcrop Yorburgh are seen at their shapeliest. Cam High Road is the Roman road running from Ribblehead to Bainbridge. On this walk you tread the easternmost section which points unerringly at Bainbridge. Even in this lower stretch the views are very good: an unrivalled length of Wensleydale can be seen, including Hawes, Askrigg and various individual features. This section is classified as a byway, so you may encounter motorised vehicles exercising their legal rights.*

Turn right to follow the arrow-like course of the Roman road - which is in good 'nick' for its age - until its eventual hi-jack by a modern road. Head up this as far as Gill Edge, just ahead, and turn left along its drive. Before reaching the houses take a kissing-gate on the left and slant right to a gap-stile at the bottom corner. A sketchy path crosses to a stile just ahead, then down to pass through an old wall and to the right of a barn. Bear right of a solid wall ahead to find a small gate in the corner beyond. The deep ravine of the Bain is just below now. Contour on above the trees, converging at the end to reach a wall-stile at the far end. Bainbridge is just below now: drop left down the steeper slope to a small gate onto a drive, heading out to re-emerge onto the green.

WHITFIELD GILL

START *Askrigg   Grid ref. SD 948910*

DISTANCE *6^{3}4 miles (11km)*

ORDNANCE SURVEY MAPS
1:50,000
Landranger 98 - Wensleydale & Upper Wharfedale
1:25,000
Explorer OL30 - Yorkshire Dales, North/Central

ACCESS *Start from the village centre, roadside parking and car park at top end. Served by Leyburn-Hawes bus.*

A richly varied walk whose highlights are two superb waterfalls

Askrigg is a wonderfully different village: formerly a market town and a famous clock-making centre, it gradually gave way to Hawes as centre for the upper dale. Its heart still recalls those days: the market cross of 1830, the three-storey houses along the main street and 15th century St Oswald's church. A striking feature internally is the roof with its splendid old beams; the font bears the marks of hinges from the 17th century days when it was locked to prevent the theft of Holy Water for Black Magic rites! There is a shop, tearooms, bakery, pottery and three pubs, the White Rose, Crown and Kings Arms. A Temperance Hall of 1906 includes the WCs, and alongside is a former Wesleyan Chapel of 1878.

Follow the main road in the Hawes direction out of the bottom end of the village, and after the last house on the left take a track down the near side of an animal feeds works. *Addlebrough's flat top breaks the skyline ahead.* From the gate at the bottom pass between the supports of a former railway bridge, and the main track ends at a sewage works. Go straight ahead on a green track, through a gate/stile and further stiles to approach stepping-stones on the river. Instead of following it to the very bank, go left on a low embankment to a small gate in a corner. Follow the fence away from it (parallel with the Ure) to a stile by a gate, from where the river is finally gained in predictably calm mood. Now accompany it downstream, a lovely stroll to emerge onto a road adjacent to the characterless Worton Bridge. *With its pub the Victoria, the hamlet of Worton is a five-minute detour just across it, up the slope.*

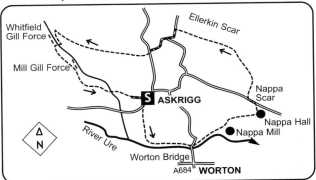

Without crossing the bridge, continue down-river from a stile opposite. After a pair of footbridges on Askrigg Beck and Newbiggin Beck in close succession the river bends off to the right, and you cross to a gate/stile at Nappa Mill Farm. Take the farm road left, re-crossing the old railway just before it crosses Newbiggin Beck by a stone-arched bridge at a ford. Without crossing, take a stile on the right and climb diagonally away on a green track. Through a corner gate, continue to a gate admitting to the foot of a rough lane rising to Nappa Hall. *This superb fortified manor house of the once influential Metcalfe family dates from the 15th century. It now operates as a farm, and in season a stunning display of snow-drops carpets the immediate wooded neighbourhood.* Follow the rough drive up past the farm buildings and out onto the road.

Turn left along the road only as far as the first branch right at a small green, signposted 'no through road', and head up through the hamlet of Nappa Scar. Remain on this lane which at the top of the hill becomes roughly surfaced. *The views now become very extensive, the fells on the south side of the valley ranging from*

Penhill to Addlebrough, and Wether, Dodd and Widdale Fells. The track swings left for a long and pleasurable level march to empty onto a narrow road climbing out of Askrigg. Turn down towards the valley, ignoring in turn a road left, a track right, and then the Muker road right. Just below is another walled track, and this you follow along to the right.

Remain on this rough way known as Low Straights Lane to its very terminus, and here escape by a stile on the left: Whitfield Gill Force at once makes its presence known through the trees directly below. Your route must take a circuitous course in order to stand at its foot, for the steep slopes deter a direct descent. Instead the path heads downstream high above the wooded beck before dropping to a footbridge, then rises to meet the path to the waterfall. Turning upstream, care is needed as the final steps can be slippery underfoot. *The scene is worth the effort however, for this is a spectacular plunge into an impending amphitheatre. Though not as tall as the better-known Hardraw Force just up-dale, some of its aspects rate it finer, not least of all the fact that it's free!*

To resume the walk retrace steps to the junction and keep straight on the wooded bank top to a stile. The way then drops to the left through more open surrounds, crossing a bridleway and another stile and along to a stile out of the gill's confines where you ignore a footbridge just below. Advance on a couple of fieldsides outside the wooded gill's boundary wall, soon returning to the action at a stile ahead. The return path runs once more along the top of the steep, wooded bank, passing an old limekiln. A junction marks the detour to your second waterfall: the situation is a near-replica of the one experienced further up the beck. *This time, however, it is but a brief stroll along a much firmer path upstream to witness the delights of the equally impressive waterfall of Mill Gill Force. Although the two waterfalls occupy similar settings in deep wooded gorges, their characters are vastly different. The first having been a straight drop, while the latter is a staircase of ledges.*

After admiring the cascades return to the junction of paths and continue downstream on an excellent path on the top side of the wooded gill. *The bonus of a distant view across Wensleydale is added to the charms of the gill itself.* From a stile at the bottom of

the wood another quickly re-enters to access a small footbridge on the beck. Just a short way downstream the path parts company with the beck to pass to the left of a mill conversion, and under a simple old aqueduct to a stile alongside. A neat flagged path runs from here across the field to join a lane, which runs along to the left to re-enter Askrigg.

Whitfield Gill Force

Opposite: Nappa Hall

45

IVY SCAR & THE URE

START *Aysgarth   Grid ref. SE 011887*

DISTANCE *7^{1}4 miles (11^{1}2km)*

ORDNANCE SURVEY MAPS
1:50,000
Landranger 98 - Wensleydale & Upper Wharfedale
1:25,000
Explorer OL30 - Yorkshire Dales, North/Central

ACCESS *Start from the National Park car park at Aysgarth Falls, east of the village. Aysgarth is served by Leyburn-Hawes bus.*

Very easy walking with contrasts between riverbank and hillside

Aysgarth is famed for its Upper, Middle and Lower Falls, where the Yoredale series of limestone makes its greatest showing to create a water wonderland. It is the grand scale of things rather than the height that provides the spectacle. What makes all this truly beautiful is the setting - thickly wooded with rich plantlife. Leave the car park at the opposite end to the entrance, and a well-used path leads down to Yore Bridge, viewpoint for the Upper Falls. *Originally from the 16th century, its graceful single-span has since been widened: Yore is the older name for the River Ure. The large building adjacent to the bridge is a café and craft shop in a former spinning mill awaiting restoration.* At the right corner of the mill by cottages a path climbs to the churchyard. *St Andrew's was restored in the 19th century, and the tower base of this very large church remains from medieval times. Inside are two fine 15th and 16th century screens.* Follow the church drive right to rejoin the road. *Just up the hill are the Palmer Flatt pub and Falls restaurant.*

From a stile across the road an intermittent path crosses the fields, keeping generally level and squeezing through a multitude of identical, quality gap-stiles on this villagers' church path. On the edge of Aysgarth the way becomes briefly enclosed to cross one last field corner to join a back lane, which leads up to the Methodist chapel on the edge of the village green. *Aysgarth village stands high above the river, aloof from the natural attraction that brings visitors in their hordes. There is a spacious air about the place, and a small green flanks the main road which divides the village. Village pub is the George & Dragon, while there is also a tearoom, with war memorial and stocks on the second green.*

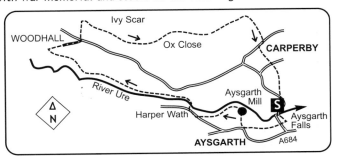

The point of arrival is also the point of departure, through a narrow gap between houses on the right. A path descends through two stiles and down a wallside, using a stile in it to drop half-right to another before dropping to the former Aysgarth Mill. A stile on its left deposits you onto its access road, which is followed left. When it turns sharply to climb the hill, leave by a stile on the right: beyond a barn another stile gives access to a pleasant path through trees by the riverside, emerging to continue to a stile where road and river converge. Head along the road a short distance to Harper Wath where a long, narrow footbridge conveys you across the Ure. *Ivy Scar's tilted escarpment forms an impressive backdrop.*

Head away on a tarmac path past scrub to reach an open area. Here a small gate set back on the left marks the commencement of a long, easy stretch along the quiet riverbank. Cylindrical concrete stepping-stones assist across an early sidestream. *Table-topped Addlebrough is distinctive ahead, while the grassy embankment of the old railway is equally distinct just to your right.* This pathless trek clings to the river through open pasture, a delightful stroll to become temporarily confined beneath the old railway. On emerging remain with the wall, crossing a small beck as the wall parts company before reaching a gateway ahead, your last link with the river. Continue on beneath the bank to the next stile to join an enclosed farm track, and turn up through a former railway bridge. The improved lane rises past West End Farm and through the hamlet of Woodhall, becoming enclosed before rising out onto the Carperby-Askrigg road. *Strung along its short lane Woodhall is almost hidden in a surround of greenery, and it has connections with the old hunting forest of Wensleydale. A filling station stands to the right.*

Cross straight over and pass between barns and house to take a farm track up the steep field. *Addlebrough rises across the dale above the hamlet.* Towards the top opt for the right branch to a gate just ahead. The day's climbing is complete as a good level track runs to the right, initially between walls. *Ivy Scar rises ahead, with the broad expanse of Penhill beyond.* Through a gate it runs to a ford/footbridge on a beck, with the fine waterfall of Disher Force plunging below you. From a gate behind the bridge, the track of Oxclose Road heads across Ox Close Pasture to old lead mines under the tilted cliff of Ivy Scar. *Ox Close has seen its share of activity in days past: the mining remains are there for all to see, while by the path further on is the site of a hut circle.* As the firmer track swings left to the old mines, keep straight on a grassy track ahead, rising away past the end of the site. Keep left at a fork to rise to a brow beyond the end of the scar, revealing further scars set back. The way runs on to eventually arrive at a gate in a wall. Don't continue up but remain on the main way swinging right towards a wall, running on alongside it to a gate in the far corner.

Carperby shortly appears ahead, with Aysgarth opposite. Now a better defined, part-embanked cart track slants down through a field into the environs of an old quarry. *Alongside are piles of flag-stones, mined and cut but then abandoned.* Through a gate the track falls to join a wall below, and remain on this good green way which runs unbroken along the top of the wall. *Bolton Castle appears impressively ahead.* Ultimately reaching a gate at the far end you join a firmer, enclosed track. Go right, part way along becoming surfaced to drop down into Carperby. *This is one of the most attractive and least spoilt villages in the dale, all its stone dwellings lining the road running through. Standing well back from the valley bottom, it was once of greater importance as testified by a sizeable 17th century market cross at one end of the narrow green. At the opposite end is a group of chapels which have been succumbing to modern trends: these include a Methodist chapel of 1820 and a Friends' Meeting House of 1864, also the old school. It is said the Wensleydale breed of sheep was first named here.*

Turn right along the main street as far as the Wheatsheaf Inn, and take a gate opposite to enter a slender field between houses. Keep on as far as a stile on the right, then continue on a similar field and along to emerge via a stile onto a farm road, Low Lane. Cross straight over and follow a wall away to a corner. *Penhill presents an imposing profile straight ahead.* From the stile a faint path strikes half-right through several fields, passing beyond a barn on a knoll up to the right, diagonally across through a stile and on to a corner one. Cross to one ahead then through one last field to enter Freeholders' Wood. Advance a few strides to join a firm path, going right and then forking left to run through the trees to a small gate onto a road. Turn left, under the old railway bridge, and the falls car park is immediately on the right. To round off the walk in style, a gate just across the road gives speedy access to the Middle Falls. *The Lower Falls could also be added by continuing on the main woodland path downstream (visited on WALK 14).*

By the River Ure below Woodhall

BISHOPDALE VILLAGES

START *Aysgarth* *Grid ref. SE 011887*

DISTANCE *6¾ miles (11km)*

ORDNANCE SURVEY MAPS
1:50,000
Landranger 98 - Wensleydale & Upper Wharfedale
1:25,000
Explorer OL30 - Yorkshire Dales, North/Central

ACCESS *Start from the National Park car park at Aysgarth Falls, east of the village. Aysgarth is served by Leyburn-Hawes bus.*

> *A gentle walk on fieldpaths around the villages at the foot of Bishopdale, culminating on the quiet side of Aysgarth Falls*

Aysgarth is made famous by its Upper, Middle and Lower Falls: here the Yoredale series of limestone makes its greatest showing to create a water wonderland. It is the grand scale of things rather than height that provides the spectacle. What makes all this truly beautiful is the setting - thickly wooded with rich plantlife. Leave the car park at the opposite end to the entrance to find a well-used path leading down to Yore Bridge, viewpoint for the Upper Falls. *Originally from the 16th century, its graceful single-span has since been much widened. Yore is the older name for the River Ure. The large building adjacent to the bridge is a café and craft shop in a former spinning mill awaiting restoration.* At the right corner of the mill by cottages a part-stepped path climbs to enter the churchyard. *St Andrew's church was restored in the 19th century, and only the tower base of this very large church remains from medieval times. Inside are two fine 15th and 16th century screens.* Follow the church drive right to rejoin the road. *Just up the hill is a pub, the Palmer Flatt, and the Falls restaurant.*

From a stile across the road an intermittent way runs across the fields, keeping largely level and squeezing through a multitude of identical, high-quality gap-stiles on this villagers' church path. On the edge of Aysgarth the way becomes briefly enclosed to cross one last field corner onto a back lane, which leads up to a Methodist chapel on the edge of the village green. *The village of Aysgarth stands high above the river, aloof from the attraction that brings visitors in their tens of thousands. There is a spacious air about the place, and a small green flanks the main road which divides the village. Village pub is the George & Dragon, while there is also a tearoom, with war memorial and stocks on the second green.*

Head along the main street to where the road drops out of the village. *On your left is an intriguing Edwardian rock garden.* Remain on the Thornton Rust road, and leave almost at once by a stile and narrow way between houses on the left. *To the left is a Quaker burial ground of 1703, with a handful of gravestones.* Into a field, rise up the wallside to join a track. Continue up through a gate/stile and on to another on the brow. *Penhill looks imposing ahead.* The grass track advances to a barn ahead, passing left of it to a gate/stile in the corner. Instead of following it to the next barn, shadow the left-hand wall to a stile at the end. Rising gently away, bear left to merge with a wall to a stile at the far corner, then on to another just ahead. Heading away, a part sunken path quickly forms above an oft-dry side valley, curving left down to a stile onto a road at Tomgill Bridge. *Opposite is a fine inscribed boundary stone.*

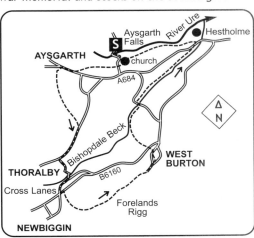

51

Turn right and enjoy big views over to Penhill as you descend into Thoralby. *This is a pleasant, less touristy village than many of its Wensleydale counterparts. It retains its pub the George, and features attractive old cottages and neat greens. At the central junction is a former Methodist chapel of 1889, and next to the Post office/shop a memorial hall of 1887.* Turn left at the main junction and along past a pinfold to Low Green: keep right to drop past a converted mill to Mill Bridge on Bishopdale Beck and right to the B6160 at Cross Lanes. *Alongside is the old school, currently a bunkhouse, up to the right is the Street Head Inn, while along the road opposite is Newbiggin.*

Your way goes left a few strides along the main road to a stile on the right. Head up by a hedge and tiny stream, and continue up two further fields, bearing slightly right to a stile onto the grassy track of Ox Pasture Lane. From a stile opposite contour left across the field to a prominent stile. From here on the way is punctuated by a regular line of stiles, each visible from the previous one. *Glorious views look out across Bishopdale to Thoralby and over to the main valley, featuring Bolton Castle and then Penhill.* In time a barn is reached on a little ridge, and from a small gate to its right converge with a tiny stream and resume in its company, a track forming to quickly enter Town Head at West Burton by way of a farmyard. Advance down the full length of the village. *For a note on West Burton see WALK 15.*

Keep left at the shop, and as the road becomes enclosed go down until a gate/stile send a short-lived way between houses on the left. This drops back down onto the B6160. From a gate almost opposite cross the field centre to a barn ahead, and from a gate to its left bear right to a corner stile at the far end. Go briefly downstream with Bishopdale Beck to another stile, cross to a wall-end near the beck, then away with the wall. After an intervening stile cross the field to a stile onto the road by Eshington Bridge, dating from 1883.

Cross the bridge and turn immediately downstream. This time cling to the beck, soon passing through Westholme caravan site, with new wooden lodges above. On leaving you pass the attractive confluence of Bishopdale and Walden Becks. *Two follies can also be seen over to the right, while far ahead is Bolton Castle beneath the moors.* Beyond a farm footbridge you are deflected left to a stile onto the A684. Go right for a couple of minutes to approach Hestholme Bridge, but without crossing turn left at Hestholme's drive. However, immediately take a stile on the left and cross to the far corner to gain a wooded bank high above the Ure.

Turn upstream through stiles, soon dropping almost to the water's edge. This is a delectable corner, with a long, low waterfall being a charming prelude to Aysgarth's Lower Falls. At a stile just beyond them the path is deflected up above the craggy, wooded bank that is forming, and you run on higher above again. As you pass through stile and gate in partnership, there are splendid views of the crashing Lower Falls below your bank of stately beech trees. The path is deflected higher above a steeper bank by a crumbling wall. *This knoll makes a good viewpoint with Penhill and Castle Bolton prominent.* With the Middle Falls visible ahead, bear left from the high point of the bank with a fence to the left corner of a wood across the field. A stile leads to a path running through it, emerging at the other end to find the church neatly-framed just ahead of you. Cross the field to it and pass along the churchyard path. To complete the walk, turn down the path past the tower to finish the walk as you began.

Falls on the River Ure at Aysgarth

CASTLE BOLTON

START *Aysgarth*   *Grid ref. SE 011887*

DISTANCE *7^{1}4 miles (11^{1}2km)*

ORDNANCE SURVEY MAPS
1:50,000
Landranger 98 - Wensleydale & Upper Wharfedale
1:25,000
Explorer OL30 - Yorkshire Dales, North/Central

ACCESS *Start from the National Park car park at Aysgarth Falls, east of the village. Aysgarth is served by Leyburn-Hawes bus.*

> *Easy walking to visit two of the valley's most famous features, one natural, one the work of man*

From the car park return to the road and turn left under the old railway bridge. Within a few strides after the station yard take a hand-gate on the right to enter Freeholder's Wood. A path rises through the trees, crossing a staggered junction with a broader path to a hidden stile just behind. A string of quality stiles in largely crumbling walls point the thin path half-right through lovely grassy pastures. After bearing well to the right of a small island barn on a knoll (with a first glimpse of Bolton Castle over to the right), turn left from a corner stile to follow a wall along to a stile onto a farm road, Low Lane. Carperby village appears just ahead. From a stile opposite pass through a long, narrow field, and from a stile on the right just short of the end, resume on another slim field to a gate onto the road in Carperby, opposite the Wheatsheaf Inn. *For a note on Carperby see WALK 12.*

Turn right a short distance past the village hall and head up Hargill Lane on the left. This rises out of the village to become a broad, walled track. *Good views look up-dale to Addlebrough.* A little beyond a barn it starts to climb away and swings left in front of an old limekiln, but here fork right on a grassier, part sunken track climbing by a wall and round to a gate/stile. A large tract of colourful pasture is entered, and with Bolton Castle in view, your near-level approach is well appraised. *Penhill looms to the right.*

A generally clear grassy track heads on through the bracken of Bolton West Park: keep left on the main way at a very early fork. Reaching a gate at the far end, the track crosses often-dry Beldon Beck and through a vast, reedy pasture close by the right-hand wall to a gate in it just short of the corner. The continuing clearer track runs above the replanted confines of the beck before passing through a gate on the left to run on to farm buildings. It continues on the access track heading away through a number of fields towards the imposing bulk of Bolton Castle. *Penhill dominates things over the valley, and the views become more open as the fields drop away.* Through a belt of woodland the track leads to the castle walls.

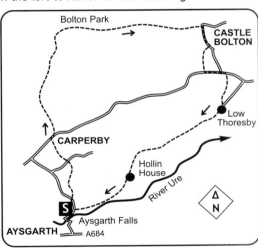

Bolton Castle is a majestic ruin that cannot fail to impress. When approached from distance it initially belies its ruinous state. This 14th century manor house was converted into a castle by Richard, the first Lord Scrope. Mary Queen of Scots was a famous guest, being imprisoned here from 1568 to 1569. The castle and its facilities are open to visitors, its labyrinthine interior being well worth exploring. Tearoom and gift shop are modern day essential additions. Though only the village has the 'Castle' prefixing the

'Bolton' *the castle often gets the same treatment. Comprehensively overshadowed by its castle, Castle Bolton village is appealing in its own right. A spacious green separates two intermittent rows of cottages, many of which long ago housed lead miners. Today this is a peaceful place, which like Carperby is well up from the valley bottom. The church of St Oswald stands almost at the castle wall. Dating back more than 600 years, this tiny place of worship reveals a surprisingly spacious interior. There are WCs at the car park.*

Between church and castle you emerge onto the village street alongside the green, and from this corner descend the road out of the village. When it swings left part way down, continue straight down a drive past barns, descending to two houses and the defunct railway: in a small cutting stands the old station house. Across the old line a largely enclosed, leafy snicket drops down to join a road. Go left only as far as the Castle Bolton junction, then take a stile on the right. Cross to one at the far left corner of the long field, then bear right to another in the very bottom corner. Just below it is a stile onto Thoresby Lane at a stone slab footbridge on Beldon Beck. Along to the right the road quickly ends at Low Thoresby.

At a gate to the right of the farm the lane is reborn as a super green path. *Centuries old, it feels little altered, and its snaking route between hedgerows is a joy.* It finally terminates just beyond a wet junction with Watery Lane. *A stream emerges from the field to run a part-channeled course over the lane: the left branch goes down to a ford and stepping-stones on the Ure.* From a gate/stile into a field a grassy track follows the wall on your left through pleasant rough pasture to a gate/stile at the very far end, with High Thoresby just over to the right. *Big open views again look over the valley: Castle Bolton is seen beneath the moors further back.* Rise gently away with the wall on your right as far as a stile in it, from where bear left over the brow to a stile near the far corner.

A grassy path bears left to a gate onto a farm road: drop left down to Hollin House. *Mighty Penhill is a major feature of the lower dale, and from this vicinity it is in particularly dominant mood.* Take the first gate down above the house, and maintain the slant across to a grassy track slanting away from a gate, and on to a gate into a large, rolling pasture. *There is a glimpse of Aysgarth church tower above the trees ahead, while in the trees below you might hear the lower falls.* Cross straight over to a bridle-gate into scattered Freeholders' Wood, from where a path runs by a fence. Emerging from the trees, turn left down to a stile at the terminus of the waterfalls path at the Lower Falls. *Aysgarth is made famous by its Upper, Middle and Lower Falls, where the Yoredale series of limestone makes its greatest showing to create a water wonderland. It is the grand scale of things rather than the height that provides the spectacle: what makes this truly beautiful is the setting - thickly wooded with rich plantlife. A distinctive cleft in the cliffs permits a cul-de-sac descent to a water's-edge vantage point.*

Back at the stile a well-trodden path heads up-river, passing by a circular detour to a more intimate viewpoint for the Lower Falls. The main, upper path climbs steps to a gate out of the trees to pass along the wood top, while the viewpoint path does likewise to rejoin further on. Re-united, the path advances to re-enter woodland, and runs on to arrive at a tiny detour down to the Middle Falls viewing platform. *Freeholders' Wood was purchased by the National Park to preserve its future, and coppicing was re-introduced.* Only a few strides further you emerge onto the road just below the car park entrance. To include the Upper Falls turn down the road to Yore Bridge, from where a path then leads back up to the car park.

Bolton Castle

WALDEN VALLEY

START *West Burton   Grid ref. SE 017866*

DISTANCE 6^3_4 *miles (11km)*

ORDNANCE SURVEY MAPS
1:50,000
Landranger 98 - Wensleydale & Upper Wharfedale
1:25,000
Explorer OL30 - Yorkshire Dales, North/Central

ACCESS *Start from the village centre, ample parking alongside the greens. Served by Leyburn-Hawes bus.*

An intimate, near-level exploration of an unfrequented valley

The Walden Valley is one of the least known and least changed in the Dales, helped by it being a dead-end for motor vehicles. Not only that, the quiet lanes that set off up each side fail to connect again, thus denying a circular tour. Individual farms are the only settlements up-dale of West Burton. The beck flows a good 7 miles to reach the village, being born under the summit of Buckden Pike. West Burton is a gem of a village, not only well away from the main road through Wensleydale but also hidden from the lesser one that runs through Bishopdale to join it. The Fox & Hounds pub and a Post office/shop/tearoom face onto an extensive green: an obelisk of 1820 stands on market cross steps, with village stocks nearby. Round the back are delightful waterfalls in a wooded dell.

Depart the village green by a narrow road left (ascending) signed to 'Walden only'. Climbing to a brow it brings good views of the valley you are to explore, backed by Burton Moor. When it forks take the left arm towards Walden South, and shortly after a barn take a stile on the right. Follow the wall away as far as a stile in it: here begins a long, largely intermittent path across the fields sloping down to Walden Beck. Mostly level, the ensuing amble requires little description: every intervening wall is graced with a stile. The first deviation occurs after a good mile, beyond a long rougher pasture with a stream crossing midway, when a wall corner deflects you half-right immediately after crossing a tree-lined stream. From a stile just up from the corner beyond, cross a fence-stile just above and cling to the perimeter of a fenced enclosure, rising with it at the far end (not as per map) to a gate/stile at the top corner. Just beyond, a hand-gate accesses a tiny footbridge over wooded Cowstone Gill. Pass through a stile to the right, on past the house and over its drive to a gate opposite: through it another drive is quickly joined to run to Hargill Farm.

Again don't enter, but in the corner just beyond a stile sends you over a tiny beck to a hand-gate, to resume a level march across the fields to join the drive of Bridge End. At this most distant point of the journey take a stile just beyond the buildings, then double back beneath them to cross a farm bridge on Walden Beck. On the opposite bank pass through a stile on the left, and continue downstream to a fence-stile. Now forsake the beck by climbing half-right to a gate at the top corner. From it turn left to begin a long, level march complementing that of the outward leg. *Bolton Castle is seen directly ahead across the main valley*. Once more virtually pathless, the only difference on this section is that gates have replaced all but one stile as very minimal height is gained. Before long the farm of Whiterow appears ahead: pass along the front of the buildings, from where its drive leads out onto a

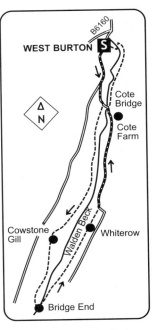

narrow road. Turn left to follow its traffic-free course back down the valley. *At a patch of open ground immediately before reaching*

Cote Farm, note the remains of a chimney that was part of the Burton Smelt Mill, serving late 17th and early 18th century lead mines. A long mile after joining the road you arrive at Cote Bridge over Walden Beck.

Without crossing, take a gate on the right to accompany the beck downstream to reach a footbridge over it. Again forgo the crossing, and this time head half-right away from it to a stile in a tiny section of wall. Rise up the side of the next field to a stile halfway, then cross to a stile right of a gate. With the isolated house of Riddings to the left, head straight across three further fields: beyond this a track descends left, but you branch right off it to a stile before it drops to a gate. Follow the wall away to a corner, and remain with it round a second corner to run left to a stile by a barn. An enclosed path now descends into the wooded environs of the beck, and steps lead down to a footbridge below West Burton Falls, which can be fully appreciated at closer range before turning right to emerge back into the village centre.

Above: Smelt mill chimney, Cote Farm   ***West Burton Falls***

UNDER PENHILL

START *West Burton   Grid ref. SE 017866*

DISTANCE *7¹2 miles (12km)*

ORDNANCE SURVEY MAPS
1:50,000
Landranger 98 - Wensleydale & Upper Wharfedale
1:25,000
Explorer OL30 - Yorkshire Dales, North/Central

ACCESS *Start from the village centre, ample parking alongside the greens. Served by Leyburn-Hawes bus.*

Exceptionally easy walking on Penhill's lower flanks: superb views

For a note on West Burton see page 58. Follow the road back out of the village to the B6160, and go right on a raised causeway to quickly turn off over the arched Burton Bridge. Head along the narrow lane past Flanders Hall on the left (note the barn), losing its surface and rising above Howraine Farm. *Your track of Morpeth Gate is an old green road used as a packhorse route. Already there are fine views ahead to Ivy Scar above Carperby and Bolton Castle: as the way improves, flat-topped Addlebrough appears behind.* Ignore a first path signed left to Temple Farm, and during a second rise look for a gate on the left signed Templars' Chapel. A path heads along the field, and through a gate at the end resumes along the top of the wooded bank. Though not always clear underfoot, this well-defined course runs for a lengthy spell to meet an enclosed track rising from Temple Farm. Directly across it is the Templars' Chapel. *The chapel of the Knights Templar is a little less exciting than it looks on the map. Here the low ruins of the chapel of the Penhill Preceptory include several graves, the structure itself dating from the early 13th century.*

Resume as before along the fieldside, interrupted only by crossing another firm, enclosed track: several wall-stiles are met. *A brief open section exploits the view over the dale. Castle Bolton, Preston and Redmire sit beneath their scars beyond Swinithwaite Hall directly below you: these are overtopped by higher moorland.* Reaching a stile onto the main road, don't use it but bear right up to a stile in the wall ahead. *The dark wall of Penhill rises steeply above now.* Bear right across the brow to the far corner where a stile admits to the right edge of a small wood. Emerging at the other side go on a short way to a stile before the corner, emerging alongside an equestrian establishment. From a corner stile to the left cross a field to a stile onto the road at the edge of West Witton: turn right into the village. *For a note on West Witton see page 67.*

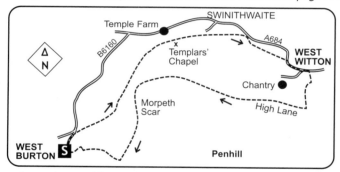

Leave by a public garden opposite the Wensleydale Heifer. By the little pond a snicket runs between high walls into a field. Bear left to a stile, then slant up to a gate/stile in the next hedge. Don't use but turn up the fieldside to the top corner. A stile admits to the trees and a path slants up the bank. At the top is a fork: go left a few strides to a stile, then continue away with a line of trees to the head of grassy Watery Lane. From a stile opposite, cross the field to a corner stile by a tiny stream and rise steeply with it to a stile onto High Lane. Turn right along the firm track of this old, walled road, which will remain underfoot for a good two miles. *Views look across to Castle Bolton, Redmire, Preston-under-Scar and Leyburn Shawl. Virtually dead-flat, all is plain sailing, indeed all the way back if desired, this being the continuation of Morpeth Gate.*

At a junction with a similar lane from the right turn to look up at the quarried face of Penhill, set back much higher above. The way resumes between broader verges to quickly reach its high point. *This is a fine moment as Wensleydale appears outspread in front.* A little further another branch joins from the right. Your lane drops down and runs on to a fork. A stark choice: uphill or downhill! *A direct finish goes steeply down to the right, rejoining the outward route.* The finest finish takes the track making a slight pull left above the bold Morpeth Scar. *From the edge is a fine bird's-eye view of West Burton, with Bishopdale beyond.* The track soon becomes enclosed as Hudson Quarry Lane, a superb, dead-straight grassy way. At its demise a continuing wallside green way resumes through rough pasture, through an intervening gateway to arrive at a wall-corner and guidepost. This is the emphatic turning point of the footpath. *Up behind are the scars of old quarries. This is a superb viewpoint with West Burton again seen in bird's-eye fashion below. Forelands Rigg divides the Walden Valley and Bishopdale.*

A clear green path doubles back down to the right past a cairn, locating a stile in the wall below. Immediately below is a steep drop, but the path takes evasive action by invoking good zigzags to reach a stile directly below. From it bear very briefly right to a stile into the top of Barrack Wood. It drops left down the bank, briefly out of the trees then down again through an old stile and a short way down the left edge of the wood. At the first corner is a fork: take a stile out of the trees and a path descends the field centre, past a wall corner down to a stile alongside a barn. An enclosed path now descends into the wooded environs of Walden Beck, and steps lead down to a footbridge below West Burton Falls, which can be fully appreciated at closer range before turning right to emerge back into the village centre.

At the Templars' Chapel

PENHILL BEACON

START *West Witton*   *Grid ref. SE 061883*

DISTANCE *5^{1}2 miles (9km)*

ORDNANCE SURVEY MAPS
1:50,000
Landranger 98 - Wensleydale & Upper Wharfedale
Landranger 99 - Northallerton & Ripon
1:25,000
Explorer OL30 - Yorkshire Dales, North/Central

ACCESS *Start from the village centre. Careful roadside parking, with a large lay-by at the Leyburn end. Served by Leyburn-Hawes bus. •Open Access, see page 8.*

A grand climb to a fine viewpoint, using some superb old tracks

For a note on West Witton see page 67. Leave by a lane at the west (Aysgarth) end of the main street by a small, grassy triangle of land opposite an old milestone. Leaving the last of the dwellings behind (noting a cottage of 1724) it climbs beneath a wooded bank to the entrance to Chantry caravan park: go straight ahead and the lane becomes an enclosed track (Green Gate) to rise past an old quarry. *Penhill forms a long skyline above, with Castle Bolton across the valley.* It soon runs more level to a junction with a splendid green road known as High Lane. Cross to a gate/stile in front and head away on a good green track, rising through two more gates to emerge onto a plateau on the open country of Penhill Quarry.

A green path heads left before you quickly fork away from the wall to cross to the most distant of four prominent spoil heaps. At any point you could opt to go right for a short-cut up to the nearest of these: alternatively go part way, and double back right at a cross-paths at the fourth ex-wall. If venturing to the last spoil heap then double back along the tops of the other three. At the right-most of these a path rises as a sunken way above it. It continues a little further then doubles back uphill to commence a surprisingly easy dog-leg climb to the edge of Penhill's summit plateau. *With Black Scar to the right and Penhill Scar to the left, this expertly engineered sunken way was built to transport sleds of peat from the moor.* Ignore the gate and turn left along the wall to a hurdle-stile, continuing on a sketchy path along the edge. The Ordnance Survey column stands over the wall as you forge on before dropping gently to another stile where a sturdy felltop wall crumbles away down the bouldery scarp on your left. Just two minutes beyond is the raised mound of the beacon site: from here the tip of the big cairn on Penhill End is seen, and a broad path bears right to it. *A fine feature of this view is the full length of Coverdale leading the eye to Great Whernside overtopping Little Whernside.*

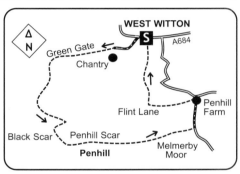

Penhill is Wensleydale's best-known fell, its ability to stand out in views from afar being greater than its popularity as a climb: its abrupt northern edge renders Penhill easily identifiable from most parts of Wensleydale, and is a regular feature of views west from the North York Moors. Penhill's own virtues as a viewpoint are assisted by the dramatic plunge of the Scar, the top of which gives near bird's-eye pictures of the lower dale. It is the aforementioned advantages which have given the hill historical significance. It was the site of a beacon, one of a chain which when lit could rapidly spread warning of some impending danger such as the Spanish Armada. Less certain is that this was the location of an Iron Age chief's last resting place. Strictly speaking, the true summit is a mile south-west of the Ordnance column, but an hour's return plod is not recommended. To clarify what exactly is what on the summit

plateau, the true top is 1814ft/553m high, the OS column is at 1725ft/526m, and the mound (the beacon site) is 1684ft/514m. To the east, and a little lower still, is the big cairn on Penhill End.

Your descent bridleway should be very clear as it drops to run through pastures below, left of the moor. A broad path drops directly from the cairn to the first gate, initially steep then merging into the true line of the old bridleway en route. *This is the self-explanatory Middleham Peat Road.* Through the gate the track begins a splendid march gently down through a succession of gates in parallel walls, only fading in the final field. Keep straight on, passing an old bield (sheep shelter) to reach a gate onto the Melmerby-West Witton moorland road. Turn left down it to soon reach Penhill Farm. At the road junction here turn left along an enclosed track known as Flint Lane.

Its level course is trodden as far as a second stile on the right a short distance beyond a prominent clump of trees, from where a trod descends a steep pasture to a stile onto a similar green lane (High Lane again). From the stile opposite a path drops above a lively little stream to a stile alongside it, then across a further field to a stile onto a third and final green lane, Watery Lane. Head directly away with a line of trees to a stile into the top of a wooded bank, and a good path slants right down to emerge into a field, with the village just ahead. Descend the hedgeside as far as a gate/stile in it, then bear left to a corner stile and on again to one final corner one, where a snicket winds between houses to emerge alongside the green opposite the Wensleydale Heifer.

Penhill Scar

REDMIRE FORCE

START West Witton   Grid ref. SE 061883

DISTANCE $6^1{}_2$ miles ($10^1{}_2$km)

ORDNANCE SURVEY MAPS
1:50,000
Landranger 98 - Wensleydale & Upper Wharfedale
Landranger 99 - Northallerton & Ripon
1:25,000
Explorer OL30 - Yorkshire Dales, North/Central

ACCESS Start from the village centre. Careful roadside parking, with a large lay-by at the Leyburn end. Served by Leyburn-Hawes bus.

Easy walking includes the valley's best long section of riverbank

West Witton is a pleasant village split by traffic rumbling through: it looks out across the valley from high above the river. It is perhaps best known for the burning of Owd Bartle, when an effigy is gleefully burnt in Guy Fawkes fashion. This occurs on the Saturday nearest St Bartholomew's feast day in late August. Bartle is said to have been a sheep thief who was hounded across the flanks of Penhill: a mosaic trail traces the course of the chase. St Bartholomew's church hides down a back lane: it retains a 16th century tower. There are two pubs, the Fox & Hounds and the Wensleydale Heifer, a Post office/store and a Wesleyan Chapel of 1842 with a Sunday School of 1884.

From the centre turn along a side road (between the two pubs) signed to the church. It drops steeply right beneath the church where you double back right on a rough lane beneath the eastern end of the village. Just before rising to the road, go left on the more inviting enclosed way of Back Lane. *On descending note stately Bolton Hall in graceful parkland on the opposite bank;*

Preston-under-Scar sits high above. Behind you is Penhill, while Bolton Castle can be seen over to the left. Twisting, turning and narrowing, this mercurial footway leads steadily downhill towards the river. At its demise don't use the gate in front, but opt for a stile on the right. In the field adhere to the left-hand boundary until it doubles sharply back left at a minor bank above a flat pasture just short of the river. Advance a little further then double back across the centre of this flat pasture on a trod to a gate in a wall. Across the stream behind, ignore a grass track heading away, and drop to a stile to gain the riverbank. Plain sailing now ensues as the Ure is accompanied up-dale through a succession of quiet pastures. *Bolton Castle is seen straight ahead, with Penhill up to the left.*

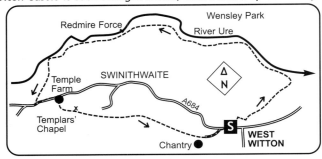

Despite its size Wensleydale only attracts large numbers to its river at a short stretch at Aysgarth. This much less-known section provides outstanding company for several beautifully wooded miles. Beyond the large, wooded Batt Island the way forges on over small knolls to a tree-clad brow above a sharp, lively bend. Dropping to cross a tiny stream, a wall soon intervenes, and a little further completely deflects you from the river. Follow it through a pasture with distinctive grassy hummocks to reach a ladder-stile. A little path continues through a much smaller second pasture to a small gate into the wooded riverbank. A path runs through the trees, and almost immediately Redmire Force greets the eye. *Keep young 'uns on a tight rein on this vantage point. The splendour of this scene is the scale of the Aysgarth-like falls on this wide section of river, not to mention the wooded surrounds and general lack of fellow humans!* The path drops to the very edge of the upper fall.

No sooner has the path deposited you at the falls then it's away again, forsaking the river to climb steps to a small gate out of the trees. Head away right along a pronounced bank to a stile opposite, then a short-lived path continues on a longer pasture, bearing right towards the end to a corner stile. Advance on outside the wooded bank top, before long emerging onto an open bank high above the river. *This is a lovely moment as the Ure winds below, with Bolton Castle stood proud on the slopes beyond.* A fence leads on to three stiles in quick succession, the middle one a wall-stile. From the third cross an extensive pasture to find a gate in the right-hand corner. A path drops through trees to briefly rejoin the river at a lovely spot alongside stepping-stones at a ford, Slapestone Wath. Ignore the stones in favour of the gate/stile alongside. Forsake the river and follow the wall curving away left, and a partially enclosed track materialises to join a drive just short of emerging onto the main road. *Alongside is an old Aysgarth/Leyburn boundary post.*

Being wary of traffic, turn left up the hill. *Part way up is an old milestone.* Leave by a stile on the right just short of Temple Farm. *In the trees opposite is a roadside belvedere, built in 1792 by the owners of nearby Swinithwaite Hall.* From the stile follow a grassy track running to the top end of the field. A gate puts it into a belt of woodland, slanting stonily left up through it to emerge onto the level. A stile on the left gives access to the remains of the Knights Templars' Chapel. *The chapel of the Knights Templar is a little less exciting than it looks on the map. Here the low ruins of the chapel of the Penhill Preceptory include several graves, the structure itself dating from the early 13th century.*

Now slant left up the field, a grass track forming to rise to a gate above the left-hand, lower wood. Continue up, meeting another track to run on to a hard access track. Turn steeply right up this only as far as a bend right, then bear left up a grassy track to the field top. *Penhill appears directly above.* From a gate/stile in the angle of the wall cross a level pasture on this distinctive shelf to the left-hand of adjacent gates, and a grassy track follows a wall on the right. Part way along take a stile in it onto the terminus of Langthwaite Lane. *Nearby Nossil Scar has replaced Penhill, which will soon return more fully.* All is plain sailing as this superb grassy footway leads between walls all the way back to West Witton. Towards the end it meets a narrow road to descend into the village.

BOLTON HALL

START Redmire   Grid ref. SE 046912

DISTANCE 5³4 miles (9km)

ORDNANCE SURVEY MAPS
1:50,000
Landranger 98 - Wensleydale & Upper Wharfedale
Landranger 99 - Northallerton & Ripon
1:25,000
Explorer OL30 - Yorkshire Dales, North/Central

ACCESS Start from the village centre. Reasonable parking around (but not on!) the village green. Served by Leyburn-Hawes bus.

> Very easy walking through the lush pastures of the lower dale

Redmire sits just outside the National Park, but its attractive green and attendant houses are equal to many within. Upon the green is a pillar erected to celebrate Queen Victoria's Golden Jubilee in 1887. Village pub is the Bolton Arms, and there's a Post office/store. From the green turn down the main road in the Carperby direction (up-dale). At a sharp bend right, go straight ahead on Church Lane: immediately fork left for a few minutes' stroll along this cul-de-sac to the church. *En route the slopes of Preston Spring are up to the left, and Penhill more dramatically across the valley. St Mary the Virgin's is a delightful little church in peaceful seclusion. Dating from the 12th century it features a splendid carved Norman doorway and a simple bell-cote. The churchyard is a riot of snowdrops at the back end of winter.*

Back on the lane, return just as far as the overflow car park and take a narrow stile on the left. Double back left across the field to another stile onto Well Lane, a hedgerowed track. Go left to the second sharp bend, and as it goes right to a lone house, advance straight on through a gate/stile, past a barn into a field. Head away with a stream to the far end, and from the slab and stile the way is identified by successive gap-stiles to approach West Wood in Bolton Hall grounds. In the last field a faint green way slants up to a tall iron kissing-gate into the trees. Just ahead is a junction of carriageways. Go straight ahead on one merging into a better one from the left, then forging on into the trees. Before long the track drops gently away, with some fine vistas over the Ure to Penhill. Emerging from the wood the track runs on a fieldside to a junction with a firmer drive, and Bolton Hall just ahead. Though your way turns up left, advance for a minute along the drive to appraise the frontage. *Bolton Hall was for three centuries the seat of the once influential Scropes, the Lords Bolton.*

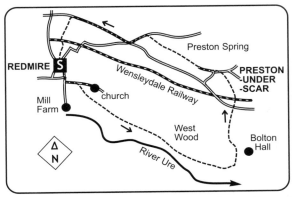

Back at the junction turn up the firm track past Home Farm, bearing left at the top and then continuing uphill at a junction to rise to a road opposite a house at Stoneham. Cross straight over and up steps to a small gate into a field, with Preston-under-Scar outspread just ahead. Cross to a gate accessing the railway line in a minor cutting. *For more on the Wensleydale Railway see page 82.* Across, bear gently left up the field to a stile left of a small barn. Bear left again up the field to find a stile in front of modern houses at the topmost corner. A snicket rises up onto a drive and thence the road. Go left along the street, keeping straight on when the through road turns down to the left. *Preston is an unassuming*

place, with a tiny triangle of green watched over by St Margaret's tiny church almost lost in the row of houses. Up to the right is a hall dedicated to six parishioners who fell in the Great War. At the end of the street a drive takes over, and beyond a few bungalows take the branch right. This is left at once by a hand-gate to its left, keeping to the upper path between new plantings and along a house front. At the end the woods of Preston Spring are entered and a fenceside path runs on through the trees. Emerging with a scrubby bank up to your right, keep on to a stile onto a road at the end. *High to the right is the gleaming limestone of Redmire Scar.*

Descend to a junction where ignore the main road and go right along an almost hidden byway. *You enjoy stunning views over to Penhill, Bishopdale, over Redmire and ahead to Castle Bolton.* Beyond a gate good verges lead on above a bank: on becoming fully unenclosed, ignore footpath signs not shown on the map. Advance on, crossing Barney Beck at another gate and reaching another path sign. Here turn down to the left alongside an old wall to a stile at the bottom of the bank. Head down the hedgeside, and in the next one keep right of farm buildings to find a stile into undergrowth. Just below, it crosses straight over a track and reaches the railway line and sidings. *Redmire's station is just along to the left: in 2004 this re-opened as the present terminus of the Wensleydale Railway.* Cross and continue down, to the bottom corner of the next field then down with a stream to a stile into the edge of the village. Head down the drive to emerge back onto the green.

Bolton Hall

UPPER COVERDALE

START *Carlton   Grid ref. SE 068847*

DISTANCE *6^{1}2 miles (10^{1}2km)*

ORDNANCE SURVEY MAPS
1:50,000
Landranger 98 - Wensleydale & Upper Wharfedale
Landranger 99 - Northallerton & Ripon
1:25,000
Explorer OL30 - Yorkshire Dales, North/Central

ACCESS *Start from the village centre. Street parking between the village hall and pub, and car park with honesty box at the hall.*

> *Tiny hamlets in the upper reaches of a peaceful side valley*

   Coverdale is easily the longest of the Ure's many side valleys: the sparkling River Cover joins the Ure below Middleham. The road out of the valley head leads over Park Rash to Kettlewell, and was part of the coaching route from London to Richmond. Earlier still, it was used by visitors to Middleham Castle. A famous son of the dale was Miles Coverdale, who first translated the Bible into English. For a note on Carlton see page 76.

   Leave by following the main street rising towards Town Head at the top end of the village. As the road swings left to leave, take the 'no through road' straight ahead. At once the lane starts to climb, quickly reaching a bend where a rough track forks right. *The view up-dale leads to the Whernsides on the skyline.* Remain on the surfaced road (a bridleway) which runs a near-straight course for some time. When it loses its surface and swings sharp right to climb away, take a gate in front and continue along a farm road. This crosses to pass right of a house, and on a field further. As it swings left to drop to East Farm, your way is the green track through a gate straight ahead. Continue with a wall through two reedy pastures, dropping left at the end to a gate/stile into a grassy enclosure. The path forks here: your way takes the green track crossing to a gate/stile at the far end. A track of sorts crosses this reedy pasture to a gate/stile in the wall ahead. It is by now clear you are heading into the side valley of Fleensop. A thin path crosses to the little stream of Turn Beck just ahead, across which is a stile by a barricaded gate.

A thin but clear path rises away onto grassy moor, a grand stride shadowing the stream down to your right. At the end this fades as you reach a gate/stile ahead. Bear a little left through dry reeds and resume along the gentle brow, a thin path continuing to a stile in the next parallel wall. *Good views look down-dale to the Scrafton moors and Great Roova Crags.* Now drop left to pick up a grass track running left to a gate in the wall (the right of way passes through then goes right to the gate at the far end) and follow the track up along the wallside to a gate in it near the far end. It runs round the field corner, but part way down leave by a gate on the right and follow a fence towards barns. Drop left to a gate beyond the nearest one, and head away on its access track. This runs into the Fleensop Valley to approach the farm at Fleensop. Crossing Fleemis Gill double back left on the surfaced road away from the farm, and rising away, quickly leave by a gate in the wall on the right.

Ascend the steep pasture to a stile at the top-left corner above a conifer block, one of many in this side valley. A grassy path then ascends rough moorland, through dry reeds alongside a wall. Just short of the top it veers right to gain the ridge wall as a broad track comes down from the right. *Little and Great Whernsides appear at the head of Coverdale, which itself increasingly rapidly unfolds.* Through the gate an intermittent track heads away through reeds. As they fade it drops a little more markedly through moor-grass as the valley floor returns to view. Between closer walls a clearer way forms, dropping left to slant pleasantly down to a gate/stile in the bottom corner. An enclosed way now drops infallibly with a wooded beck to emerge quite suddenly into Horsehouse. *The dale's first sizeable community is a compact huddle of grey buildings: these include the cosy Thwaite Arms and St Botolph's church of 1869.*

Turn right only as far as the pub, then take a lane behind it for a short way to leave by dropping down a small lawn to a gate below. Descend a small enclosure to the next gate into flat fields. Bear left to another gate and cross to a hand-gate right of a barn. The River Cover is now joined and, ignoring an early footbridge and later a stone-arched farm bridge, is accompanied downstream for a mile. Part way along as you emerge from a sidestream bridge into a large open pasture, ignore a Gammersgill guidepost and remain on the open bank, curving increasingly pleasantly around with a wooded bank opposite. *Penhill sweeps into view during this stage.* After a gate/stile at the end it is vacated at the second solitary stile with a crude ford alongside, crossing diagonally to a gate/stile in line with a lone house beyond (ignore farm buildings to your left). Continue towards the house, bearing right to a hand-gate well to its right. A part wooded enclosure leads onto the road in Gammersgill, a farming hamlet with a classic Norse title.

Go right on the road out of the hamlet, soon leaving by a stile on the right. Bear left to another onto Turnbeck Lane, a narrow green footway enclosed in greenery. At its terminus you emerge via a footbridge on a sidestream: cross the field to an outer wall-corner and on a pleasant green way to the top far end of the next pasture. Through the gate advance on above a wooded bank falling to the river, and straight on to a footbridge on a stream beneath a small wood. From a corner stile just beyond continue away, crossing a stile part way on to a stile onto a narrow road. Head up this just as far as the next bend, then take a stile to cross a field bottom. From the next stile head for one in the top corner, then go right again to another corner one. Again slant up to a corner one at the end, then cross to successive gates in intervening walls into a wooded dell. Rise a few paces left on a grass track then drop to a footbridge. Without leaving the confines take a thin path left up by the wall to rise the short way to a stile onto a farm track, with the road in the village just above. *A motte site is to the left as you join the track.*

COVERDALE HAMLETS

START Carlton   Grid ref. SE 068847

DISTANCE 6$\frac{1}{2}$ miles (10$\frac{1}{2}$km)

ORDNANCE SURVEY MAPS
1:50,000
Landranger 99 - Northallerton & Ripon
1:25,000
Explorer OL30 - Yorkshire Dales, North/Central

ACCESS Start from the village centre. Street parking between the village hall and pub, and car park with honesty box at the hall.

Unsung fieldpaths link tiny villages in a peaceful side valley

Carlton-in-Coverdale (Sunday name) is one of many linear villages in the district, and here the string of houses seems almost endless. The village features the Foresters Arms, the tiny church of Christ the Good Shepherd, and a Wesleyan Methodist chapel of 1873. A pronounced grassy knoll behind the pub at Round Hill is the site of a motte, an early wooden castle of which little is known. From the vicinity of the village hall head up the main street past the pub. Shortly after, a footpath goes off left along a drive at a tiny sloping green. Continue up however, to reach the Methodist chapel. Just a little further on the right is Flatts Farm, which bears an inscription relating to Henry Constantine, the Coverdale Bard. Almost back at the chapel, turn right down an enclosed footway by a seat, that runs by a tiny beck round the back of the houses. As it meets a drive (the earlier path branch) take a stile on the right.

Here you are immediately out in the open, with a long wall of moorland stretching across the other side of the valley, leading from the Scrafton moors and Great Roova Crags up towards the Whernsides at the dalehead. Double back across the field to the next stile, continuing through a handful of first-rate gap-stiles to emerge onto a road corner. Without treading tarmac take a gate on the left and descend to a prominent stile at the bottom. *Just across the valley note some superb examples of strip lynchets (early farmers' cultivation terraces).* Bear right from this to a corner stile, then on the fieldside to join narrow Cover Lane. Turn down this to Nathwaite Bridge, a fine single stone-arched structure over the River Cover.

Immediately across, turn right on a wooded drive above the river. Just after it bends away a path turns off left up a small wooded bank, up stone steps to a stile putting you in a sloping pasture. Follow the grassy track rising left, passing an old limekiln before it fades. *Big views*

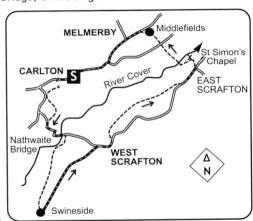

look back over the valley to Carlton under Penhill. Maintain this course to the top to find a redundant stile just behind. Rise away briefly to a fence-stile behind, from where head straight across the field to a stile in a section of wall opposite. Resume across the field, meeting the start of a wall further on. Follow it as far as a gateway in it near the far end, then rise briefly left to a stile where wall and fence meet. A faint path rises across a larger pasture, slanting up with the aid of waymarks towards a house at Swineside. *The Whernsides dominate impressively over the bleak dalehead.*

The way fades but continue rising to a very short length of wall corner, where a stile awaits. Head along the fenceside to another stile into a garden. Cross to the right of the house, past another and then into a yard at Swineside. From a gate at the end join the terminus of its surfaced access road. *This isolated hamlet comprises a good half-dozen dwellings.* Double back left up this for a short spell on grassy moorland, quickly passing through a cattle-grid to head for West Scrafton. *Massive views from this fine promenade feature Great Roova Crags just to the right, also looking down the valley and across to Carlton under Penhill.* A gentle descent only drops down at the very end to reveal West Scrafton at your feet.

Joining the through road turn right into the village. *Note the bee-boles in a garden opposite.* Keep right to reach a small green. *West Scrafton is well off the beaten track and looks more than happy to remain so. The tiniest of greens sits amongst attractive houses, including the Manor House and the little Methodist Chapel built as a Primitive Methodist Chapel in 1866. Seat, phone box, Victorian postbox and a little tap all add their contribution. A house set back from the earlier, lower green bears a 1689 date-stone. The bridge, meanwhile, sits astride a dark ravine, while just across it the fellside falls all the way to the village as tracks head off over the moors to both Colsterdale and Nidderdale.*

Cross to the far corner of this little green where a rough access track terminates in a grassy area between houses. Drop right, a path entering the wooded ravine of Caygill Scar. The path drops down this enclave, over a footbridge on a mill-cut and emerging onto the end of another access road at another tap. Turn right on the continuing access track, and almost at once a path drops right from it to rejoin Caygill. Passing through a stile you trace the gill a short way down through a field to a farm bridge. Cross this and the field behind to a stile and steps onto a corner of an enclosed track, Low Lane. You meet it at a junction with an old sunken way, so rise a few strides right to the lane proper and bear left on it as it rises very gently away, improving into a fine green way. At its demise keep straight on the fieldside through a gateway, and cross to a gate ahead. *A prow of Braithwaite Moor rises ahead.* Now bear right to find a stile in the tiniest section of wall in the corner, then sharp right to a similar arrangement, with gate, alongside a tiny tree-lined stream.

Cross the stream and contour left across the field to the deeper, wooded Thorow Gill, where a footbridge eases the crossing. *Note the original old slab below.* Up the other side bear right across the field to a stile onto a back road. Go left for a few minutes to a junction with the access road into the hamlet of East Scrafton. *Across the valley Penhill End rises prominently above Melmerby.* On the left a gate/stile send you down the fieldside to a bridle-gate into the wooded banks of the Cover, and a part-stepped old path slants down to the riverbank. *A big old limekiln stands on the left, while on the right the site of an ancient ford is evident as an old hollowed lane, now unusable, drops down to the river.* The main feature is the forlorn yet atmospheric ruin of St Simon's Chapel by the river. *It was actually dedicated to St Simon and St Jude, and is thought to be over 600 years old. Immediately upstream is a lively spring which exists for the briefest of flows before joining the river: this is St Simon's Well, a holy well of great antiquity itself.*

A path heads upstream a short way past the well and beneath low scars to St Simon's Bridge (modern footbridge) on the river in a nice corner. On the other side go right a few paces to a stepped path doubling back up through Scar Wood. From a stile at the top rise left up the field to a stile, and continue directly up two fields onto a road. Go right several paces to a gate and head up the field to the barns of Middlefields. A stile to the right of the barns puts you onto a track, turning left on it past the buildings and up onto a higher road. Turn left here to quickly pass two junctions, the second at the foot of Melmerby village. *Melmerby is a peaceful farming settlement on the lower slopes of Penhill. On the corner is an 18th century guidestone, while the house on your left was the Topham Arms pub until 1960. Up the street are Manor House Farm and a humble Methodist chapel of 1893 furtively tucked round the back of a house.* Keep straight on the road to another junction which marks the beginning of straggling Carlton.

Looking back to Carlton and Penhill from Swineside

22

LEYBURN SHAWL

START Leyburn   Grid ref. SE 112904

DISTANCE 6^{1}4 miles (10km)

ORDNANCE SURVEY MAPS
1:50,000
Landranger 99 - Northallerton & Ripon
1:25,000
Explorer OL30 - Yorkshire Dales, North/Central

ACCESS *Start from the market square in the centre. Ample car parking. Served by bus from Ripon, Masham, Richmond and Hawes.*

A very easy walk with the renowned Shawl preceding old lead workings, parkland, a charming village and lovely fieldpaths

The busy little town of Leyburn is Wensleydale's true gateway. A vast market place fulfils its original function on Fridays, when dalesfolk from miles around add further colour to the scene. At the top stands the imposing town hall of 1856, while pubs and cafes do brisk trade. Just off the market place are 18th century Leyburn Hall, Thornborough Hall, St Matthew's church of 1868, and the Roman Catholic church of St Peter & St Paul, dating back to 1835. The town has a Tourist Information Centre and is home to the Wensleydale Show in late August.

Leave the market place by the old town hall, crossing the top road to Commercial Square, with the Bolton Arms on the left. At the top of the small square, 'Way to the Shawl' signs send you up a side street, turning left at the top to emerge via a kissing-gate into the edge of a field. Head away along the immediately forming grassy edge, the start of the Shawl. *Leyburn Shawl was laid out as a place of promenade in 1841, a typical Victorian Sunday afternoon attraction. This initial stretch is popular with dog walkers, while there are seats galore from which to appraise the immediate view of Penhill across the dale.* Advance along the edge, modest limestone outcrops appearing as the path runs on through several of them above the woods. On entering the trees the finest, longer section now begins, enjoying panoramic views over the dale. The path forges on and the situation constantly improves, with a sheer scar beneath your feet creating breaks over the trees to make more of the view. The presence of a vast quarry over to the right is made largely immaterial thanks to a high wall.

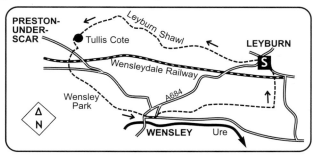

Eventually the trees, and with them the Shawl, end. The path drops down a little to a stile and kissing-gate out into a large sloping pasture, with truly spacious views looking to Penhill and beyond. Slant down the field to a kissing-gate at the bottom, then across to another. Bear left to a nearby fence corner that encloses the banks and ditches of an ancient settlement and field system. A track forms to turn down through a gate in the wall below, and runs down to a junction with a firmer track above Tullis Cote Farm. Bear right to the farm and along to a crossroads of tracks at the end of the buildings. Note the fine four-arched building ahead. Don't cross to the driveway past it, but turn sharp left down the outside of the farm buildings. At the bottom corner, advance straight on down a fieldside track to a gate below. It then drops left through the remains of Keld Head smelt mill. *Built to serve an old lead mine, the buildings are still very evident despite dense undergrowth. Most prominent is the tall, square chimney, while on your right is an arched level that penetrates deep into the hillside.* The track doubles back right past a house to emerge onto a back road.

At the road first look right to see the beautifully converted, three-storey Preston Mill. Cross to the gate opposite and across to the railway line. *The Wensleydale Railway was a 40-mile link between the Vale of York and the Pennines, reaching Hawes in 1878 and on to Garsdale Head (then Hawes Junction) where it met the Settle-Carlisle line. The last passenger service ran in 1954, and the rails were removed above Redmire in 1965. The lower 22 miles remained to serve a quarry above Redmire, but in 1992 this ceased and only an occasional military train brought armoured vehicles towards Catterick Garrison. A campaign to save the line has made remarkable progress, with passenger services re-starting in 2003 from Leeming Bar as far as Leyburn, extending to Redmire just a year later. Just along to the left is the former station.*

A grass path crosses the field behind to a bridle-gate onto a road. Go left for a couple of minutes then take the first footpath into trees on the right. A path runs to meet a driveway junction: go straight ahead on the one rapidly leaving the wood. It runs along above the wood top (note the wooded ravine) to approach a house. Don't cross the cattle-grid but deflect a few strides left up to a fence corner. A few strides further is a bridle-gate which sends a path down outside the grounds of the house to another bridle-gate into the vast expanse of Wensley Park, in the grounds of Bolton Hall. The invisible path slants gently down the parkland pasture, ultimately gaining the main drive at a bridle-gate just short of the far corner. Go left to immediately join the road in Wensley. *Quoits pitches are passed just before an ornate lodge at the end.*

Wensley is a delightfully attractive village, largely out of character with the typical Dales villages upstream. This is partly due to the fact that this once important market town (a charter was granted in 1202) that gave its name to the dale was decimated by Plague in 1563, and never recovered its status. Pride of place goes to Holy Trinity church with its various Scrope memorials, including their 17th century family pew: also of interest is a 16th century rood screen. The graceful bridge dates back to the 15th century, though much enlarged since. Village pub is the Three Horseshoes, while visitors are welcome at a candle-makers in the old mill. Your route enters the village at a tiny green featuring a water pump.

Across the road turn down to the right and then quickly left on the Middleham road above the church. Immediately over a bridge turn left up a back lane. At the second bend, where it turns sharp left uphill, leave by a gate on the right. Cross to one opposite then on a longer field bottom. Through a gate/stile then a kissing-gate at the end, advance on another field bottom before a lone tree points the thin path up to a kissing-gate at the top of the wood in front. *Look back at Penhill across the dale.* Head away, and part way on a stile sees you to the other side. *This is Old Glebe Field, a nature reserve of the Yorkshire Wildlife Trust where traditional farming practises are upheld.* Rise left over a tiny footbridge to a stile in the top corner. A lengthy but pleasant trek ensues through the fields, largely a direct line marked by a rich variety of stiles. Ultimately the way runs on above a barn conversion to discover the stony Low Wood Lane in a wooded hollow just beyond.

Cross straight over and resume on a pleasant bank. *Middleham is clearer ahead to the right, while above you the edge of Leyburn awaits.* From a stile at the end follow a wall away to another, and in the next field bear up to the left. Rise through successive gates/stiles with Leyburn church tower waiting prominently above. At the top an access road puts you into modern housing intruding on the line of the path. Joining a little close go briefly right to find the path preserved, an enclosed way climbing between the houses to a drive. Go up some steps in front to join a road bridge over the railway line and up onto the road opposite the church.

Preston Mill

COVER BANKS

START Middleham   Grid ref. SE 127877

DISTANCE $5^3 4$ miles (9km)

ORDNANCE SURVEY MAPS
1:50,000
Landranger 99 - Northallerton & Ripon
1:25,000
Explorer OL30 - Yorkshire Dales, North/Central
Explorer 302 - Northallerton & Thirsk

ACCESS Start from the town centre. Ample parking in the square and also higher up the top end. Served by Ripon-Leyburn bus.

Very easy walking based on the beautifully wooded lowest reach of the River Cover, with attractive bridges and old pubs

Middleham is an absorbing town: a village in size perhaps, but unquestionably a town in stature. It is famous for both its horse-racing connections (numerous stables nearby) and its castle, and is the historic gateway to Wensleydale. The castle ruins dominate, finest features being the massive Norman keep and 14th century gatehouse. It was for centuries the stronghold of the Nevilles, and known as the 'Windsor of the North'. Richard, Earl of Warwick - the King-maker - lived here, and his daughter married Richard, Duke of Gloucester, later to become the much-maligned Richard III, and the castle's most famous resident. The castle is cared for by English Heritage and is open to view.

A cross at the head of the town recalls the grant obtained in 1479 for a twice-yearly fair and market by Richard, when Duke of Gloucester. Alongside are a jubilee fountain, the old school of 1869, and a fine sundial of 1778 on a house. The parish church of St Mary & St Alkelda dates back in part to the 14th century, and *includes a monument from about 1533 to Abbott Robert Thornton of Jervaulx. Adjacent are the three bays of Kingsley House, a former Rectory dating from 1752. Centrepiece of modern-day social life is the small sloping square, surrounded by pubs and tearooms. There is a village store, chippy and one or two more shops. Another market cross stands here on ancient tiered steps, from where one can daily witness elegant horses being lead up onto or back from the grassy moor to exercise on the gallops. Considering the rich appeal of the place, tourism has barely taken hold, and the little town maintains a genuine atmosphere of its own.*

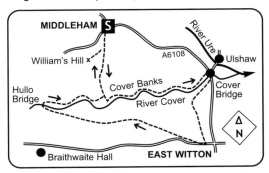

Leave the main street by making for the castle. Pass to its left and along an enclosed track along the left side of the castle walls. Emerging into a field at the end, head straight on up the wallside, over the brow and down to a corner gate/stile. Resume down the wallside past a barn. *Ahead, the deep environs of the River Cover await, with Braithwaite Moor behind and Penhill further right.* A path forms as you descend almost to the riverbank. Becoming more wooded at the bottom, this is a fine moment as the river rolls beneath the dark wall of Cover Scar. Before the bottom a path bears left to slant down to join a lower one just above the river. Turn left and head downstream, the path soon entering woodland, and then climbing above the river before dropping back down to leave the wood for open pasture. Remain on the very bank to find a good path reforming to enter a shorter woodland stretch by the rocky bank. This soon emerges to run on to some stepping-stones. *Though not used, a dozen massive blocks tempt a near-foolproof crossing.*

Resuming down your bank take a stile in front, soon after which a stile puts you into the wooded riverbank. The way is now clear and most enjoyable as the path clings to the river to reach the pub at Cover Bridge. At the buildings you are deflected left to a stile onto the road. *Just along to the left are Ulshaw Bridge and church (see WALK 24).* At Cover Bridge the homely Cover Bridge Inn perches on the riverbank: cross the bridge to steps on the right down to the riverbank. Cross a stile onto the very bank opposite the pub garden, but instead of following the Cover upstream, stay with the hedge as it curves round to the left. Go on to a gate/stile at the end, then on to another gate/stile just ahead. Here a guidepost sends a path right towards the stepping-stones, but your way heads directly on, through a gate in a fence and on to a stile by a modern barn. Pass round the back to a stile then go left with the wall. Maintain this line until on a minor brow East Witton appears ahead. In a smaller enclosure take a stile on the left at the end of the hedge, and head along the last field to emerge into the village street.

East Witton suffered terribly in the Plague of 1563, and was rebuilt as an estate village by the Earl of Ailesbury in the early 19th century. The church of St John the Evangelist, built in 1809, stands just east of the village. The two lines of houses are set back from a vast, sweeping green, which features a quoits pitch and an old water pump. High up the green is an old Methodist chapel of 1882, and also a little Post office. At the main crossroads stand the Blue Lion pub, an attractive former school and a working tap embedded in a boulder. Leave by turning right along the street, and at the end of the green a narrow road heads out of the village. Almost at once take a stile by a gate on the right. Two invisible paths head away: one goes to the stepping-stones, while yours bears left to a stile at the far end. Continue with the hedge on the right through two further fields to join grassy West Field Lane. Turn right along this leafy pathway to it demise at a small wood. From a stile in front a good path runs along the left side of the wood.

Emerging into a field at the end advance straight on, and at the next gateway a farm track forms. When it turns left through a gateway towards East Witton Lodge, leave it and stay on another wallside track. *Penhill is well seen ahead, with Braithwaite Moor up to the left.* A gate at the end puts you into open pasture: remain with the hedge on the right. When this kinks, slant across to rejoin it and remain with it past a small farm building to pass through the old hedge further along. On the other side continue on to the very corner. Here a stile then footbridge crosses a tiny stream to emerge into a big pasture. A faint trod bears right over the centre to a gate in the opposite corner. Now overlooking the river again, either advance along the top of a wooded bank, or drop down the bank to follow it along to the bridge. Towards the end drop down to reach delightfully located Hullo Bridge. *This stone-arched bridge sits among some splendid river scenery as the Cover runs through a modest ravine and over a slabby limestone bed.*

Across, take a stile on the right and head downstream. Almost at once the path climbs the wooded bank into a field. Resume along the bank top, all the way on to rise to a slim plantation. Twin stiles send a brief path through it to resume along the wood top, with views down to the river. As it starts to drop back down to the river, bear off left to contour across to meet the wall-cum-fence opposite. Now back on the outward route, turn up with it to be back in Middleham within minutes. *On re-entering the head of the rough lane back to the castle, a detour can be made by taking the gap-stile on the left. From it slant up the field to a gate in the fence, then continue up to inspect the prominent William's Hill. This wooded knoll is the site of a 'ring and bailey', where a timber castle long preceded the main attraction below. It consists of an outer bank, ditch and inner bank. Concealed within is a small level centrepiece, where a 40ft/12m high motte stood. Certainly its siting was unsurpassed, offering an unhindered view in all directions.*

Market cross, Middleham

JERVAULX ABBEY

START Jervaulx   Grid ref. SE 169856

DISTANCE 7 miles (11km)

ORDNANCE SURVEY MAPS
1:50,000
Landranger 99 - Northallerton & Ripon
1:25,000
Explorer 302 - Northallerton & Thirsk

ACCESS Start from Jervaulx Abbey car park on the A6108, along-side the tearooms. Please adhere to the request to support the honesty box. Served by Masham-Leyburn bus.

Easy, delightful walking through parkland and by riverbank

Returning to the road, the visitor's path to the abbey is through a gate opposite, though the public right of way is along Jervaulx Hall drive to the left, going right over a cattle-grid to intersect the abbey path in the park. The path to the abbey runs straight on. *Though perhaps best saved for the end, it is difficult not to explore the ruins at once, such is their impact on this opening section. Jervaulx Abbey is a rare specimen, one of the few in private hands: admission is by honesty box. A guidebook provides an interesting read and useful plan. Jervaulx was founded by Cistercian monks in 1156, having originated from Byland Abbey, and briefly set up near Aysgarth a decade earlier. The name is derived from Yore Vale, Yore being the old name for the River Ure. At the Dissolution in 1536 Jervaulx suffered particularly badly, and much of the stone was carted off for other buildings. The remains are in a delightful condition that would have appealed greatly to the Victorian sense of the Romantic, being less uniform than those in official care. A stone trough by the gate was a slab on which Abbots were embalmed.*

The walk, meanwhile, remains on the broad carriageway winding on through the open pasture of Jervaulx Park. It remains firm throughout, passing a very attractive pond then rising to a back road alongside a lodge. Turn left, passing farm buildings to descend to Kilgram Bridge. *This fine bridge spans the Ure by four arches, and dates back to Norman times: it straddles what is thought to be a paved Roman ford. Upstream is a fine prospect of Penhill.*

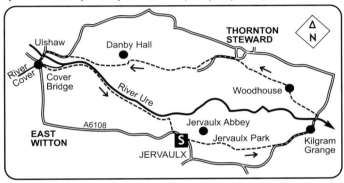

Cross the bridge and within two minutes take a gate/stile on the left just beyond a water company installation. Head away on a track to another gate/stile into a field, then slightly right across the centre to a stile in the hedge opposite. The village of Thornton Steward is your objective behind. *Over the dale are wooded Witton Fell, Braithwaite Moor and Penhill.* Head away with a hedge on the right, and through the gate at the end turn right and pass through a gateway to approach Woodhouse Farm. Through a gate/stile into a smaller enclosure, bear left to one in front of a modern barn, then go left to a gate/stile out into a field, leaving the farmyard undisturbed. Remain on the hedgeside through several pastures, then level with a small wood, slant up the large pasture to find an old stone gap-stile in the hedge ahead. Cross a couple of strip enclosures to a gate onto a driveway, which leads along through further gates and past houses to rise onto the village green.

Thornton Steward is a lovely linear village with smaller greens running its length. At the junction up above is the tiny old school of 1866. Go left along the road. Along the way you pass the old water pump and the Institute of 1925 (with WC) on the right, opposite the Manse. At the end pass through the gate signed Manor Farm and church. As the narrow road winds down to the left, a nice short-cut sees a path signed at the gate into the trees in front. A path through this narrow belt emerges into a field where the path forks. Take the left one slanting down into the trees, where a thin continuation bears right to a bridle-gate into the churchyard. *St Oswald's is a very old church with a Norman doorway and nave windows. This isolated gem also sports a 13th century font.*

A bridle-gate in the bottom corner puts you onto the rough access road. Ignore this and head away along the field top, through a gate at the end and along further fieldsides. At a kink a bridle-gate transfers you to the right side of the wall to resume through more pastures. *The parkland of Danby Hall is increasingly evident as you amble over lush turf.* When a bridle-gate transfers you back to the left side, Danby Hall itself quickly appears ahead. From a gate at the end of the fence you enter spacious grounds immediately in front of the hall. Advance on, merging into a firm track coming down from the right. This is now followed through the park beneath the front of the hall. *This large mansion of the influential Scrope family shows an impressive front dating from the 19th century, but visible on the right rear corner is a 15th century pele tower.*

The track runs on to become enclosed at Danby Low Mill. Continue along the drive past a house and the converted mill itself,

now in the company of the Ure to join a road. Go left to a junction at Ulshaw Bridge. *On the right is a lovely churchyard, behind which is the Roman Catholic church of St Simon & St Jude, dating from 1868. Its small tower is prominent in the locality, while the Scrope connection is evident with their modern descendants represented in the churchyard.* Go left over the bridge. *In its central refuge stands a stone sundial dated 1674. This fine four-arched old bridge crosses the Ure in grand surrounds.* At the junction stands the Cover Bridge Inn. *With the walk three parts done, refreshment at this cosy pub is surely merited.* Now cross Cover Bridge, the last bridge on this enchanting river. From a kissing-gate on the left head downstream on a delectable green path. Though you have hitherto seen little of the riverbank, the walk's final quarter makes amends.

The Cover's confluence with the Ure is easily missed, passed in a mix of island greenery known as The Batts, and the path now enjoys a brilliant mile and a half. *With good fortune you might see the dazzling flash of a kingfisher on this secluded reach. The broad, grass strip that separates you from the fields is maintained*

throughout. Across the river Danby Low Mill is seen then Danby Hall also makes an appearance, while later you pass an attractive fishpond formed from an ox-bow lake. Ultimately, after lingering as long as possible on these lush banks, the way ends at a gate by a small wood. *Enjoy a last look back at the winding Ure backed by Penhill high above East Witton church.* Turn up the track onto the road and go left for five minutes to return to Jervaulx.

At Jervaulx Abbey

Opposite: Ulshaw Bridge

At the road first look right to see the beautifully converted, three-storey Preston Mill. Cross to the gate opposite and across to the railway line. *The Wensleydale Railway was a 40-mile link between the Vale of York and the Pennines, reaching Hawes in 1878 and on to Garsdale Head (then Hawes Junction) where it met the Settle-Carlisle line. The last passenger service ran in 1954, and the rails were removed above Redmire in 1965. The lower 22 miles remained to serve a quarry above Redmire, but in 1992 this ceased and only an occasional military train brought armoured vehicles towards Catterick Garrison. A campaign to save the line has made remarkable progress, with passenger services re-starting in 2003 from Leeming Bar as far as Leyburn, extending to Redmire just a year later. Just along to the left is the former station.*

A grass path crosses the field behind to a bridle-gate onto a road. Go left for a couple of minutes then take the first footpath into trees on the right. A path runs to meet a driveway junction: go straight ahead on the one rapidly leaving the wood. It runs along above the wood top (note the wooded ravine) to approach a house. Don't cross the cattle-grid but deflect a few strides left up to a fence corner. A few strides further is a bridle-gate which sends a path down outside the grounds of the house to another bridle-gate into the vast expanse of Wensley Park, in the grounds of Bolton Hall. The invisible path slants gently down the parkland pasture, ultimately gaining the main drive at a bridle-gate just short of the far corner. Go left to immediately join the road in Wensley. *Quoits pitches are passed just before an ornate lodge at the end.*

Wensley is a delightfully attractive village, largely out of character with the typical Dales villages upstream. This is partly due to the fact that this once important market town (a charter was granted in 1202) that gave its name to the dale was decimated by Plague in 1563, and never recovered its status. Pride of place goes to Holy Trinity church with its various Scrope memorials, including their 17th century family pew: also of interest is a 16th century rood screen. The graceful bridge dates back to the 15th century, though much enlarged since. Village pub is the Three Horseshoes, while visitors are welcome at a candle-makers in the old mill. Your route enters the village at a tiny green featuring a water pump.

Across the road turn down to the right and then quickly left on the Middleham road above the church. Immediately over a bridge a delightful corner. Over a footbridge and old ford of Bird Ridding Wath the way rises in splendid fashion up the other side to emerge onto a back road. Go right for a long half-mile's pleasant amble, gradually rising to a junction with Caldbergh's cul-de-sac road. Turn up into the hamlet, rising past the houses until the lane ends at a gate at the top. *Caldbergh is one of a number of tiny settle-ments in this neighbourhood which remain pleasantly unspoilt.*

A firm farm track now takes up the running, and is followed left (ignore an immediate right branch) along a wallside and over several cattle-grids to the lone house at Ashes Farm. With heathery Braithwaite Moor just above, a track continues across the field, and in the next one gains a brow with long views ahead to the North York

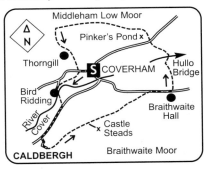

Moors. When the field boundary on your left returns the grassy way runs to a small gate in a corner recess ahead. Escaping sheep pens you enter a small tract of Open Access. Just above are the distinct banks of Castle Steads, well worth a tiny detour by slanting up to the near end to amble along the edge of the grass platform. With grassy banks and ditches, this is the superbly located site of an Iron Age fort of the Brigante tribe. Drop back to rejoin your route at a gate at the end, and as the adjacent wall drops away, head straight across to a gate in a fence. Resume across extensive Hanghow Pastures, passing the top of a slim plantation. *During this stage you have good views of the house at Coverham Abbey and, well above it, Middleham Low Moor.* Gradually declining to the far corner, a gate/stile put you onto a road. Turn right, past a farm and along to the drive of Braithwaite Hall. *This impressive triple-gabled house dating from 1667 is in the care of the National Trust.*

Opposite the drive is a gate from where a sometimes faint track heads away on a steady descent through two pastures to the River Cover at Hullo Bridge. *The stone-arched bridge sits among some splendid river scenery as the Cover runs through a modest ravine and over a slabby limestone bed.* Across, a grassy track bears left up the bank, easing out to slant pleasantly across to a gate onto the unfenced Coverham-Middleham road over Middleham Low Moor opposite Pinker's Pond. *At the site of an old quarry, the attractive pond is likely to be dry.*

Alongside a casual parking area head straight up a broad track that accessed the quarry face just above. *Big views look across the Cover to Braithwaite Moor, then Coverdale and mighty Penhill.* It turns right along the front of the quarry, but leave by a thin path at the eastern end, rising to a protective fence-end just above. Whilst you could rise a little further onto Middleham Low Moor to gain a hard track and go left, better to use a trod that runs on past the other end of the fence then enjoys a superb section above the scrubby rim of Ever Bank looking down on the pond. At the end it fades on approaching a wall: bear right up to its top corner, above which a firm track runs. You are now virtually on the crest of Middleham Low Moor. Either remain with this track all the way, or strike off across the largely pathless, short-cropped grass. While keeping an eye open for racehorses the Ordnance Survey column at 774ft/236m appears ahead, and is quickly attained. *Middleham is renowned for its horse-racing connections and the moor is the main venue for putting the elegant animals through their paces.*

The moor stretches out ahead, with fine views of Coverdale and Wensleydale divided by Penhill. A gentle drop precedes a steady amble. Reaching a pronounced dip on the left side, drop to rejoin the track by a clump of scrub: alongside is the first chink in the armour of the fine wall enclosing Cotescue Park, a gate framed by ornate posts. *Not vehicle width, it is much used for access from the stables below.* Turn down this between walls, passing the large house of Fern Gill and with an appreciable wooded gill alongside, briefly down its drive: reaching a pond take a redundant gap-stile at the start of a wall and go left of the ponds, across the grounds to a fence-stile opposite. The next stage was diverted in 2010: from the stile cross to the far corner of the field, beyond the last building at Thorngill. Passing through gates continue to one in the smaller field corner just beyond. Here a grass track is joined, and descends a superb fieldside course all the way down onto a road. To your right are the remains of a creamery, while your starting point is just along to the left.

WALK LOG

WALK	DATE	NOTES
1		
2		
3		
4		
5		
6		
7		
8		
9		
10		
11		
12		
13		
14		
15		
16		
17		
18		
19		
20		
21		
22		
23		
24		
25		

INDEX
walk number refers